Rapunzel

Book, Music & Lyrics by Jez Bond
and Mark Cameron

Published by Playdead Press 2015

A CIP catalogue record for this book is available from the British Library.

ISBN 978-1-910067-41-3

Printed by BPUK

Playdead Press
www.playdeadpress.com

PARK

Park Theatre was founded by Artistic Director, Jez Bond. The building opened in May 2013 and, with two West End transfers, two national theatre transfers and three national tours in its first two years, quickly garnered a reputation as key player in the London theatrical scene. In 2015 Park Theatre received an Olivier nomination and won The Stage's Fringe Venue of the Year.

Park Theatre is a neighbourhood theatre with a global ambition.

We present world class theatre, collaborating with the finest existing and emerging talent. We programme classics through to new writing, distinguished by strong narrative drive and powerful emotional content. We produce both in-house and in partnership with the most excellent existing and emerging producers, with whom we endeavour to provide an unparalleled level of support.

With a welcoming and nurturing environment we want Park Theatre to be accessible to everyone, within our diverse community and beyond – and through affordable ticket pricing and outreach programmes we aim to engage with those with little or no experience of theatre.

We aim to be a beacon for all and an ambassador for theatre worldwide.

★★★★★ "A five-star neighbourhood theatre." Independent

As a registered charity [number 1137223] with no public subsidy, we rely on the kind support of our donors and volunteers. To find out how you can get involved visit **parktheatre.co.uk**

For Park Theatre

Artistic Director | Jez Bond
Executive Director | John–Jackson (JJ) Almond
Creative Director | Melli Bond
Development Director | Dorcas Morgan
Assistant to the Directors | Amy Lumsden
Finance Manager | Catherine Barrow
Venue and Volunteer Manager | Naomi Dixon
Sales and Marketing Manager | Alona Fogel
Box Office Manager | Androulla Erotokritou
Box Office Supervisors | Mark Blythe, Bessie Hitchin, Katy Shearstone and Regan Shepherd
Technical Manager | Sacha Queiroz
Theatre and Buildings Technician | Mat Eldridge-Smith
Duty Venue Manager | Mark Blythe, Barry Card, Rochelle Clarke, Androulla Erotokritou and Haroula Lountzi
Creative Intern | Wanda Szwed
Cafe Bar General Manager | Tom Bailey
Bar staff | Luis Aguiar, Gemma Barnett, Grace Botang, Calum Budd-Brophy, Jack Carroll, Amy Conway, James Crocker, Robert Czibi, Nicola Grant, Philip Honeywell, Jules Moore-Cook, Joshua Oaks-Rogers, Olivia Onyehara, Sara Pau, Emma Petrusson and Katy Shearstone.
Public Relations - Arabella Neville-Rolfe and Andrew Greer for Target-Live

President – Jeremy Bond

Ambassadors
David Horovitch
Celia Imrie
Sean Mathias
Tanya Moodie
Hattie Morahan
Tamzin Outhwaite

Associate Artists
Mark Cameron
Olivia Poulet
Sarah Rutherford (Writer in Residence)
Charlie Ward

With thanks to all of our supporters, donors and volunteers.

RAPUNZEL

Book by Jez Bond and Mark Cameron
Music and Lyrics by Jez Bond*
Footnotes by Mark Cameron

CAST

Rapunzel/Queen | Aretha Ayeh
King Gerard | Rolan Bell
The Great Gazombees | Mark Cameron
Dobson/Prince Corbyn | Alex Hope
Dr Chuff | Avita Jay
All other parts played by members of the cast

CREATIVE TEAM

Writers | Jez Bond & Mark Cameron
Director | Jez Bond
Set and Costume Design | Victoria Johnstone
Choreographer | Lee Proud
Lighting Design | Julian McCready
Sound Design | Theo Holloway
Orchestrator / Musical Director | Dimitri Scarlato
Puppet Maker | Nick Ash
Casting Directors | Lucy Jenkins CDG and Sooki McShane CDG
Design Assistant | Cecilia Trono
**'Set Me Free' co-written by Awsa Bergstrom and Ian Dench*

PRODUCTION TEAM

Production Manager | Simon Dixon
Company Stage Manager | Helen Cobb
Assistant Stage Managers | Victoria Figler, Bessie Hitchin and Preece Killick
Set Builders | Tandem Set and Scenery
Producer (for Park Theatre) | John-Jackson (JJ) Almond
Associate Producer | Amy Lumsden
External Marketing | Nick Boaden for Target Live

CAST

Rapunzel/Queen | Aretha Ayeh
Theatre credits include: *Love Me Tender* (No.1 UK Tour); *Barnum* (Chichester Festival Theatre); *Dick Whittington and his Cat* (Lyric Theatre Hammersmith); *Pendragon* (Rose Theatre Kingston); *Red Hunter* (Youth Music Theatre: UK); and *Orvin-Champion of Champions* (National Youth Musical Theatre). Film and TV credits include: *Fantastic Beasts* and *Where To Find Them* (Warner Bros. David Yates); *The Quiet Ones* (Hammer Films); Russell T Davies's *Cucumber* (Channel 4).

King Gerard | Rolan Bell
Rolan Bell's theatre credits include: *Memphis* (West End Olivier nominated for best supporting actor); *We Will Rock You* (West End and 40th Anniversary International Arena tour); *Ragtime, A Midsummer Night's Dream* (Regent's Park Open Air Theatre); *Fela!*, and *Liberation Day* (National Theatre); *1936* (Arcola); *The Harder They Come* - nominated for Best Actor, What's On Stage Award (Playhouse, Theatre Royal, Stratford East and Barbican*); An African Cargo* and *An Evening of Soul Food* (Greenwich Theatre); *Carmen Jones* (Royal Festival Hall); *The Lion King* (Disneyland, Paris); *Cinderella* and *Jack and the Beanstalk* (Cambridge Arts Theatre). Television credits include: *Doctors*, series regular in *Eastenders* and *WPC 56* (BBC) and *Scott and Bailey*. Rolan also works extensively as a voice over artist

The Great Gazombees | Mark Cameron
TV credits include: regular characters in *Coronation Street, Steel River Blues, Emmerdale, Doctors* and guest roles *in Law and Order, The Royals, Waterloo Road, Casualty, Holby City, Eastenders, The Roman Mysteries, Vincent, Mayo, The Royal, The Bill, Fifty Five Degrees North, Extreme Endurance,*

Brookside.
Film credits include: *Scar Tissue, The Boss,* (Reed Festival short film winner), *The Damned United, Casanova's Love Letters, Tomo* (Sundance Film Festival Winner) and *The Other Side.*
Theatre credits include: *Hurling Rubble at The Moon* (Park Theatre, London), The DAFTAS Ceremony Host in Park Theatre Review (Park Theatre), *Sleeping Beauty* (Park Theatre), *Mathematics of the Heart* (Theatre 503 and winner of Brighton Fringe festival – Best Play), *Sleeping Beauty* (Salisbury Playhouse), *Life Imitates Art* (Camden Peoples' Theatre), *The Game of Love* and *Chance* (National Tour), *The Breakfast Soldiers* (Contact Theatre, Manchester), *The Bergman Project* (Tristan Bates Theatre), *The Country Wife* (The Gatehouse), *Blue Funk* (Old Red Lion), *The Taming of the Shrew* (Shakespeare in the Park), *Romeo and Juliet* (Cannizaro Park), *Robin Hood* (Swansea Grand), *The Pudding Pirates* (Durham Gala Theatre).
Radio: *Daniel Chadwick, Home Front,* BBC Comedy Pilots: *Horror House, Sportstalker, Barry Brown, Singed* and *Quimble, Double Act.*

Dobson/Prince Corbyn | Alex Hope
Alex graduated from the Royal Welsh College of Music and Drama. Theatre credits include: Scripps in *History Boys* (National Tour); *First Episode* (Jermyn Street Threatre); *The Witness* and *Riot Squat* (Thrive Theatre). Radio credits: *August 1914* (BBC).

Dr Chuff | Avita Jay
Avita trained at Drama Studio London. Theatre credits include: *Spare* (New Diorama Theatre), *Toad* (Southwark Playhouse), *Sunday Morning at the Centre of the World* (Southwark Playhouse, Battersea Arts Centre), *The Merry Wives of Windsor* (National Tour), *Londonee* (Rich Mix),

Secret Cinema's *Brazil, Unsung* (Wilton's Music Hall), *The Tragicomedy of Mac-Beth* (National Tour), *Warde Street* (Park Theatre), *Pioneer* (National Tour), *Peer Gynt* (Crossrail Place) and *The Man Who Found His Freedom* (The Space Theatre). TV and Film credits include: *Emmerdale* (ITV), *L8R* (BBC2), *The Rezort* (Matador Pictures) *London, Paris, New York* (Fox Star Studios) and *Twenty8K* (Formosa Films). Avita also regularly narrates audiobooks and is a reader for InterAct Stroke Support.

CREATIVES

Co-Writer / Director | Jez Bond

Jez Bond graduated Hull University with a BA Honours in Drama and was awarded the Channel Four Theatre Director Bursary, under which he trained at Watford Palace Theatre. Jez is Artistic Director of Park Theatre – which he founded. Credits for Park Theatre; *Sleeping Beauty*, *Jack and the Beanstalk* (both of which he co-wrote), *Adult Supervision* and *Hurling Rubble at the Sun*. Freelance credits include; *The Fame Game* (Tour of Austria), *Sleeping Beauty* (Salisbury Playhouse), *Oliver!* (starring Rowan Atkinson, Oxford), *I Have Been Here Before* (Watford Palace Theatre), *The Twits* (Tour of Switzerland), *Misconceptions* (Hong Kong Arts Centre), *Big Boys* (Croydon Warehouse), *Shot of Genius* (Leicester Square), *Canaries Sometimes Sing* (Kings Head & France) and *A Season in South Africa* (Old Vic). As a dramaturge he has worked with writers at Soho Theatre, Theatre Royal Stratford East, Royal Court and Young Vic

Co-Writer | Mark Cameron

Writing: As an Associate Artist of Park Theatre Mark co-writes the theatre's Christmas shows with Jez Bond the Artistic Director: *Sleeping Beauty* in 2013 and *Jack and the Beanstalk* in 2014. Both plays were published by Methuen. Mark has co-written three sitcoms currently in development, *The Lycra Ladies*, *Twiddles* and *Bonk Bonk* and *Monsters* and has co-written and performed in numerous sketch comedy shows including *Too Big To Play* with Jez Bond, *Three Men and a Squid* and *Squidfellas* (Japan tour). Mark also works extensively as a voice-over artist for television and radio.

Set and Costume Design | Victoria Johnstone

Victoria Johnstone trained at Central Saint Martins and Rose Bruford College, receiving first class honours in Theatre Design. She has lived in Scotland, Texas and the Middle East and is now based in Sussex and London.

Her other set and costume designs for the stage include *Rockston Stories (*Outside Edge, Hoxton Hall), *Our Mutual Friend* by Charles Dickens (Brighton Open Air Theatre), *The Last of the De Mullins, Ivy & Joan, Flowers of the Forest, Statements After an Arrest Under the Immorality Act, Fever,* set design for *Natural Affection* and costume design for *Saturday Night* by Sondheim and *The Notorious Mrs Ebbsmith* by Arthur Wing Pinero (all at Jermyn Street Theatre), *Fear and Misery of the Third Reich* by Bertolt Brecht (Brighton Dome), *Sarai* by Paul Anthony Morris, *Daphne* by Richard Strauss, *Origin of the Species* by Bryony Lavery and *Coming Home* by Athol Fugard (all Arcola), *Cover Her Face* - a transgender reinterpretation of Webster's *Duchess of Malfi* (Bethnal Green Working Men's Club), *Spent* and *How to Find Us* (Soho Theatre), *Unstated* and *Sense* (Southwark Playhouse), *Hotel Medea* (Shunt Vaults), set design for *The Dilemma of a Ghost* by Ama Ata Aidoo (Border Crossings / National Theatre of Ghana) and Heiner Müller's *Hamletmachine* (BAC / International tour).

Victoria also works as a costume designer in film and television.

Choreographer | Lee Proud

Originally from Newcastle Upon Tyne, Lee is an Award Winning freelance choreographer. Recent Theatre Choreography includes: *Aladdin* (Oxford Playhouse) *The Smallest Show On Earth* (UK Tour) *Grand Hotel* (Southwark

Playhouse) *The Wind in the Willows* (Grosvenor Park Open Air Theatre - UK Theatre Award nomination for Best Children's Production) *The Producers* (UK and Ireland Tour) *Billy Elliot the Musical* (Reykjavik City Theatre) The German Premier of *Ghost the Musical* (The English Theatre, Frankfurt) *Lottys War* (Yvonne Arnaud Theatre, Guildford and UK Tour) *Revolution In The Elbow of Ragnar Agnarrson Furniture Painter* (Off Broadway - Minetta Lane Theatre, New York) *Carousel* – OFFIE Nomination – Best Choreographer (Arcola Theatre London) Hairspray (Curve Leicester) *The Curious Incident Of The Dog In The Night-Time* (Reykjavik City Theatre) *Tyne* (Theatre Royal, Newcastle) *Rent* (Royal Welsh College, Cardiff) *Cooking With Elvis* (Live Theatre) *The Revenge of Sherlock Holmes* (Hoxton Hall) *Mary Poppins* (Reykjavik City Theatre) *Victor Victoria* - OFFIE Nomination Best Choreographer - (Southwark Playhouse) *Boy Meets Boy* - OFFIE Nomination Best Choreographer (Jermyn St Theatre) *Mack and Mabel* - WINNER OFFIE Award - Best Choreographer and Broadway World Award Nomination for Best Choreographer (Southwark Playhouse), *Utopia* (Soho Theatre London) *Guys and Dolls* (Upstairs at the Gatehouse) *A Northern Odyssey* (Live Theatre) Lee was an original cast member and subsequent resident choreographer of the London production of *Billy Elliot the Musical* he also assisted on the Show in Sydney and on Broadway. He lives in London. More info @LeeProud www.leeproud.com

Lighting Design | Julian McCready
As a lighting designer credits include: *Ken Campbell's History of Comedy - ventriloquism*, *The Menu* (National Theatre); *Oliver!* (Oxford); *I Have Been Here Before* (Palace Theatre Watford); *Risk Everything* (Old Ren Lion); *Canaries Sometimes Sing* (Old Red Lion & King's Head); *Hyperlinx* (Citizen's Glasgow, Pleasance Dome and Tricycle); *Wild*

Raspberries (Citizen's Glasgow and Pleasance Dome); *Adult Supervision, Sleeping Beauty, The Man Who Shot Liberty Vallance* and *The Vertical Hour* (Park Theatre).
Julian also lights and designs art installations including several large scale projects on the sides of hills using nature materials combined with lighting.
As Chief Electrician at the National Theatre until 2011, Julian has headed up the lighting departments in all three theatres and toured number productions across the world. Re-lights include *Elmina's Kitchen, Closer, Private Lives, Betrayal*, Mike Leigh's *2,000 Years*, Antony Sher's *Primo* and Katie Mitchell's *The Waves.*
As a freelancer he worked on the London 2012 Olympics as well as a number of arts festivals and corporate events – and has consulted on the technical installations at theatres both in the UK and abroad, including Park Theatre.
Julian is a professional member of the Association of Lighting Design.

Sound Design | Theo Holloway
Theo has over eighty credits as a sound designer and composer, including many of the Park Theatre's in-house productions, six seasons at the Scoop at More London, *At the Mountains of Madness, Hedda Gabler, Spring Awakening, Romeo & Juliet, Macbeth, & Hamlet* (UK Tour for Icarus Theatre), *Charley Bear's Christmas Adventure* (The Ambassador's Theatre), *Men are from Mars, Women are from Venus* (UK Tour, Edinburgh), *Gutted, Shalom Baby, The Graft, Two Women, There's Something About Simmi* (Theatre Royal Stratford East), *Third Floor* (Trafalgar Studios), *The Moon is Halfway to Heaven* (Jermyn Street Theatre), *Parade* (Southwark Playhouse), *Sign of the Times* (Duchess Theatre – Musical Arrangements), *Corrie!* (The Lowry), *A Plague Over England* (Duchess Theatre) and pantomimes for Qdos, First Family, Newbury Corn Exchange and Theatre Royal

Stratford East. He also works as a technical consultant and developer for live sound, specializing in radio frequency engineering.

Orchestrator / Musical Director | Dimitri Scarlato
Dimitri Scarlato is a Composer and Conductor born and bred in Rome where he studied Composition, Piano and Conducting at the Conservatorio di Musica S.Cecilia. In 2004 he moved to London to attend a MMus in Composition at the Guildhall School of Music & Drama and in 2014 he completed a DMus in Composition at the Royal College of Music, which in 2010 selected him as a RCM Rising Star. His music has been performed in several venues across Europe and Accademia Filarmonica Romana (institution which regularly worked with Stravinsky) premiered his chamber opera *Fadwa* in May 2013 at Teatro Olimpico, Rome.

In 2015 he won the 3rd Composition Competition at the International Spring Orchestra Festival, with his piece *Caduceo*, written for two pianos.

Regarding his film activity in 2007 he worked in the music pre-production of *Sweeney Todd*, by Tim Burton and in 2009 he composed and supervised the music for *The City in the Sky*, which has been selected at the 66th Venice Film Festival. In 2011 Dimitri has been selected at *VOX3 - Composing for Voice* workshop at the Royal Opera House of London, and at the Berlinale Talent Campus 2011 as a film composer.

In this 2014 he has been the music/conducting coach for sir Michael Caine on the new Sorrentino's film *Youth* (premiered at the Cannes Film Festival and due to be released in the UK 2016).

In 2015 he conducted his first concert at the Barbican Hall, premiering his composition *Rhapsody of Memories*, which featured the established British violin player Nicola Benedetti. In November premiered is new chamber opera *The Christmas Truce* in Rome, and on the 18th of December will be released in the UK cinemas *Sparks & Embers*, a British independent film starring Kris Marshall, for which he composed the soundtrack.

He is currently writing the soundtrack for *Thala my love*, an independent film about the "Arab spring" in Tunisia.
www.dimitriscarlato.com

Puppet Maker | Nick Ash
Nick is an actor and puppet & mask maker and has a varied career in film, TV, theatre and radio. In 2006, he co-founded the award-winning Scratch Built Productions with Geoff Smith, creating imaginative new shows, and all of the masks and puppets for their productions which include *Baby Boomers*, *Knight Time*, *How to be a Hero* and The Three Sillies. Nick has also designed and built puppets and masks for Shakespeare's Globe (*Dream Space*), Polka (*The Gorilla* and *Charlie and Lola*), Royal and Derngate (*His Dark Materials*), Pied Piper (*Robin's Winter Adventure*) Time Won't Wait (*That's the way to do it*) and Proteus Theatre Company (*Alice in Wonderland*, *The Secret Garden*, *Sophia and the Snail*, *The Mission* and last year's *Rapunzel*). After the success of last year's sell-out show *'Father Christmas's Christmas List*, Scratch Built will also be producing a new festive show for pre-school children at the Proteus Creation Space called *Santa Town*.

Casting Directors | Lucy Jenkins CDG and Sooki McShane CDG

For the Park Theatre: *Hurling Rubble at the Sun / Moon, Contact.com, Jack and the Beanstalk, The Man Who Shot Liberty Valance, Sleeping Beauty, Desdemona, Adult Supervision* and *Casualties.*

West End credits include: *The Play That Goes Wrong* (Duchess Theatre), *Bomber's Moon* (Trafalgar), *War Horse* (New London); *Carrie's War* (Apollo) and *Cool Hand Luke* (Aldwych).

Other theatre credits include: *A Christmas Carol* (Rose Kingston), *The Divided Laing* (Arcola), *Gigi* (Tabard), *All My Sons* (Rapture Theatre), *Time Plays* (Hampton Court Palace), *History Boys* (National Tour), *Wet House* (Live/ Soho Theatre), *All My Sons* and *Moon on a Rainbow Shawl* (Talawa Theatre, tour), *Our Country's Good* (Out Of Joint), *Much Ado About Nothing* (Royal Exchange Theatre), *War Horse* (UK Tour), *Solid Air* (Theatre Royal Plymouth), *The Butterfly Lion* (Mercury theatre & tour), *Serpent's Tooth* (Almeida / Talawa), *Chalet Lines* (Bush Theatre / Live Theatre), *What Falls Apart, Flying in to Daylight, Tyne,* and *Cooking with Elvis* (Live Theatre) *The Glee Club,* (Cast Theatre) and several productions for Nottingham Playhouse including *Duchess of Malfi, Rubenstein Kiss, A Skull in Connemara, Tony's Last Tape, Posh, Arcadia, Time and the Conways, The Kite Runner, My Judy Garland Life, Richard III, The Ashes* and *Diary of a Football Nobody.*

Television credits include: *Whitney – The Diva and her Demons* (ITV), *In The Dock* (RDF), *Skins* (Company Pictures), *Wild At Heart* (Company Pictures), *The Bill*

(Talkback Thames), *Samuel Johnson: The Dictionary Man* (October Films), *Family Affairs* (Talkback Thames).

Film credits include: *Twelfth Night (*Interactive); *The Comedian's Guide to Survival*; *Bliss!*; *A Special Guest*; *Only Child*; *Pulsar*; *Arthur and Merlin*; *Awaiting*; *Containment*; *Five-A-Side*; *Entity*; *The Somnambulists*; *Desi Boyz* and *H10*.

PRODUCTION TEAM

Production Manager | Simon Dixon
Simon is a freelance production manager, his previous credits include: *Roaring Trade* (Ann Pinnington Production), *Keep The Home Fires Burning* (TJM Productions), *The Man Called Monkhouse* Tour (Cahoots Theatre), *An Audience with Jimmy Savile* (Cahoots Theatre), *Dead Sheep* (Cahoots Theatre), *Cosi fan Tutte* (Opera UK) and *3 Dimensions* (RADA Youth Company). Simon previously was the Technical Manager at RADA Studios.

Company Stage Manager | Helen Cobb
Helen studied Stage Management and Technical Theatre at the London Academy of Music and Dramatic Art. Since graduating she has been touring internationally with several children's musical theatre productions and has just finished a UK tour *of Sherlock Holmes and the Ripper Murders* for Talking Scarlet Productions. This is Helen's second production at Park Theatre having recently worked on *Hatched and Dispatched* in Park 90.

Assistant Stage Manager | Victoria Figler
Victoria graduated from Bristol Old Vic Theatre School in July 2015 with a BA Honours in Professional Stage

Management. During her training she specialised in Art Direction and Prop making for TV and Theatre and has since done work within the Art Department for BBC IPlayer Shorts and with Red Production Company's 'The Five'. This is Victoria's first production with Park Theatre, and she's excited to apply her personal creativity to the team.

Assistant Stage Manager | Bessie Hitchin
Bessie trained for a year at Park Theatre as the technical apprentice and is excited to be working on her first professional production in the stage management team.

Assistant Stage Manager | Preece Killick
Hailing from the Shropshire/Welsh border, Preece trained as an actor at the Bristol Old Vic Theatre School and after 15 years of treading the boards, turned to directing and stage management and has since been involved in London based, National and International tours of plays, musicals and opera. Productions such as *La Traviata*, *Gutted*, *The Events*, *The Barber of Seville*, *Houdini*, *Romeo and Juliet*, *Carmen*, *Josephine*, *The Magic Flute*, including tours of Malaysia, Singapore and the United States. Preece is also a writer, having completed four plays, three screenplays and has just completed his first novel.

DRAMATIS PERSONAE

This musical can be performed by a cast of up to nine actors – plus, if desired, a chorus.

Below are the roles, and suggested doubling, for the minimum cast size of five.

Principals

King Gerard [male]

Queen Gerardine / Rapunzel [female]

Dobson / Prince Corbyn [male]

The Great Gazoombees [male]

Doctor Chufflebanger [female]

Fairy 1* [male]

Fairy 2* [female]

**Fairy 1 and Fairy 2 are listed in this script as they appeared in the Park Theatre production – played by puppets with their voices pre-recorded. They could equally be performed live by two actors of any gender.*

A Note on Characters

It is always difficult to find English language equivalents for Waa dialects. However, whilst the wording has not been written out phonetically, the dialogue for two characters has been written with particular types in mind. For King Gerard this is a stereotypical bumbling posh English gentleman. For 'The Great Gazoombees' this is a cockney East End of London geezer, until he adopts the persona of baron who could sound Russian or Spanish, possibly and quite ideally both at the same time. For specific details on the language of Waa and the dialect of Püss Püss please see: Histiography.

SONGS

SONG 1: JUBILATION (Act1, Sc1) – Full Company
SONG 2: THE GREAT GAZOOMBEES (Act1, Sc2) – Dobson & The Great Gazoombees
SONG 3: MALADY (Act1, Sc5) – Doctor Chufflebanger
SONG 4: PARTNERS (Act1, Sc6) – Dobson
SONG 5: WE WERE MEANT TO BE… (Act1, Sc9) – Queen Gerardine
SONG 6: HOW CAN I BE YOURS? (Act2, Sc1) – King Gerard
SONG 7: GETTING TO KNOW YOU (Act2, Sc) – Prince Corbyn
SONG 8: SET ME FREE (Act2, Sc3) – Rapunzel
SONG 9: LIGHTNING STORM (Act2, Sc6) – Prince Corbyn and Rapunzel
SONG 10: MEDLEY (Act2, Sc7) – Full Company

HISTIOGRAPHY[1]

Welcome fair reader once again to the wonderful world of Waa[2]. The third instalment of *The Chronicles of Waa* takes us to the Kingdom of Püss Püss[3]. Whereas in *Sleeping Beauty*, Pilipots[4] was the spiritual home of the flannel and in *Jack and the Beanstalk* Nowen was the spiritual home of tupperware, Püss Püss is renowned for being the spiritual home of places that have nowt special to be the spiritual home of. Püss Püss was nearly the spiritual home of the spirit level but they just couldn't work out how to get that bubble thing in the liquid so they ended up with only quite a straight stick which failed to impress the 'Spiritual Home Of…' assessment panel. The flora and fauna of Püss Püss are unremarkable but this hasn't affected their love of vegetable darts, a non-contact mime based sport that often results in death or worse; excessive chaffing of the dangling dibs. Most Püss Püssians have a keen sense of justice but no sense of smell which has all but decimated the aromatherapy industry. In terms of culture one would find more in an Aldi yoghurt – apart from Püss Püss's burgeoning phallic topiary clubs which continue to rise and rise. Finally, the use of the word trombone is considered highly offensive as are chestnut pop socks.

---

[1] See also hysterectomy, histamine, anti-histamine and Uncle Michael Heseltine.

[2] A beautiful and fertile land stretching from the notorious Gazoobian mountains in the East to the land locked Port of Quell Sang Fran in the middle of the Gazoobian mountains.

[3] A tough and unforgiving region where rivers are optional. The spiritual home of the spirit level.

[4] The beating heart and dribbling nostril of Waa. The spiritual home of the flannel. See Sleeping Beauty, Methuen 2013.

A NOTE ON PRONUNCIATION

"The language of Waa is not for the faint-hearted. The Püss Püssian dialect is the most unique in the land of Waa and has been the focus of the most vicious disagreements in the history of linguistic analysis. Whereas Des Cartes the Marxist reactionary and part time plumber declared the dialect illegal on medical grounds, Barry "the fudge" Thompson has campaigned tirelessly for a national Püss Püss Dialect bank holiday to fall just after Match of the Day but before Songs of Praise to avoid traffic congestion and marsupial indigestion. One should approach the accent with the same passion and flexibility as one would approach Lionel Blair in stormy weather. Florescent hot pants and inflatable compasses are recommended to enhance articulation but all diphthongs should be prefaced with a light smattering of oregano relish. No relish however should be afforded to adjectives which must be swallowed over-dramatically the moment they are spoken. Adverbs naturally have diplomatic immunity. Northern Püssians prefer to communicate via osmosis so a pocket salt dispenser is welcome. In stark contrast the deeply religious southerners interact with damp sponges and lace doilies. If ever in a conversational cul-de-sac there is nothing the humble folk of Püss Püss appreciate more than a stylised elbow gesture."

The above is an extract from Pecil Thrent's highly controversial haiku 'I am a shelving unit'.

LOCATIONS

All locations expect for the Market are in Püss Püss

The Royal Palace

A Market in Gwafalth[5]

The Gates of the Capitol

The Woods

Inside the Tower

Outside the Tower

[5] Region of Waa very close to itself.

<u>ACT ONE</u>
PROLOGUE

A puff of smoke and two fairy puppets appear, both with Arsenal scarfs on. They speak as parodied sports commentators, above noise of football chanting.

FAIRY 1 (V/O)
What a sensational finish there for Arsenal.

FAIRY 2 (V/O)
And an inspired substitution from the manager…

FAIRY 1 & FAIRY 2 (V/O)
…Arsène Venger

FAIRY 1 (V/O)
Well that's all we've got time for this week. Next week we'll be back for that tricky away match against West Bromwich Albion.

FAIRY 2 (V/O)
So from here in the Arsenal Emirates stadium it's good night. *[This next section is specific to Finsbury Park – and can easily be replaced with any reference local to the venue where it is being performed.]*

Final sports theme-tune music, with cheering. Over this we hear the sound of a tube train's doors opening and closing and the tube moving off…

VOICE OVER
Next station Finsbury Park.

...the sound of train doors opening....

FAIRY 1 (V/O)
Here we are in Finsbury Park. Just one stop north of Arsenal on the Piccadilly line.

FAIRY 2 (V/O)
Whilst of course the Victoria line offering local residents a speedy route into the centre of town.

FAIRY 1 (V/O)
Routes of course so vital in today's life. Routey tooty mcgrooti. Mcgwinbe jinbee jenbe.

...and the hollers of the fruit sellers beside Finsbury Park station.

FRUIT SELLER (V/O)
Taste the mango. Taste the mango. Do you like mangos? [etc]

FAIRY 1 (V/O)
Mangos being the staple diet for a Finsbury Park resident!

FRUIT SELLER (V/O)
Banana banana. Banana banana. [etc]

FAIRY 2 (V/O)

And let's not forget the humble banana.

FAIRY 1 (V/O)

Well from one arena to another as we enter Park Theatre and start our journey once again into the magical world of Waa.

FAIRY 2 (V/O)

It might be worth saying Fairy John, for those of who've not been to Waa before it really is a fascinating place, full of its own unique language and traditions.

FAIRY 1 (V/O)

I can't claim to understand it all myself, Fairy John, but my word that's a lovely dress you're wearing.

FAIRY 2 (V/O)

Today's eagerly anticipated encounter between good and evil sees Rapunzel thrust into the competitive realm of fairytales...

[Continues...]

SCENE ONE
The Royal Palace

King Gerard, Doctor Chufflebanger and Queen Gerardine wait in nervous anticipation. Centre stage, a door is prominently lit. Tension music builds.

[Continued...]

FAIRY 1 (V/O)
Our story begins in the kingdom of Püss Püss on a truly historic day. Here at the palace, the King and Queen have been trying for a child for many years, time is running out.

QUEEN GERARDINE
My family have ruled this land for centuries, I hope we've made the people happier, healthier, we have peace now. But if we don't have an heir, the neighbouring warlords will destroy all the good we have achieved.

KING GERARD
We will have a child. I know it.

FAIRY 1 (V/O)
Doctor Chufflebanger, the noble court medic, escorting the Queen there to the anti-room for the undertaking of the royal urinary-based pregnancy test.

Doctor Chufflebanger enters and escorts the Queen off through the door.

FAIRY 2 (V/O)
A hush descends as the Kingdom waits in anticipation.

Sound of wee into a toilet.

FAIRY 1 (V/O)
Well the dulcet tones of the royal wee there, performed of course by the royal We – and there she is!

Queen Gerardine emerges, waving to the crowd.

FAIRY 2 (V/O)
And now all is left in the capable hands of Doctor Chufflebanger to determine the results.

FAIRY 1 (V/O)
Doctor Chufflebanger bingy bongy of course no stranger to conception, royal or otherwise. The hopes of the Kingdom, pinned on this moment – will there or won't there be an heir?

The door opens and Doctor Chufflebanger emerges, with a pregnancy strip in her hand. Tension music climaxes.

DOCTOR CHUFFLEBANGER
(Jubilantly) Shentel[6]!

---

[6] An exclamation of joy reserved exclusively for positive pregnancy tests and successful haircuts in ancient royal families. The final 'l' is flexible.

ALL
Shentel!

DOCTOR CHUFFLEBANGER
Your majesties, you're having a baby.

KING GERARD
Get word to the warlords of Quenteth and Zambar. This kingdom lives on! This is Püss Püss.

King Gerard and Queen Gerardine are overjoyed.

SONG ONE: JUBILATION

KING GERARD
Go light the torches trailing through the forest
Go sound the trumpets high up on our walls
Ensure that all men, women, and their children
Shall know our kingdom will prosper once more

And we cry...

ALL
Jubilation at the coming of the heir apparent yes it's
Jubilation at the coming of a royal child
Jubilation throwing parties all across the land so full of
Jubilation Jubilation Jubilation
Jubilation Jubilation Jubilation

KING GERARD
Our royal lineage continues

DOCTOR CHUFFLEBANGER
The oldest family in Waa

ALL
Waa Waa Waa Waa Waa!

DOCTOR CHUFFLEBANGER
Noble and fair and just their ruling

KING GERARD
And now the people travel very far
To give their…

ALL
Jubilation at the coming of the heir apparent yes it's
Jubilation at the coming of a royal child
Jubilation throwing parties all across the land so full of
Jubilation Jubilation Jubilation
Jubilation at the coming of the heir apparent yes it's
Jubilation at the coming of a royal child
Jubilation throwing parties all across the land so full of
Jubilation Jubilation Jubilation
Jubilation Jubilation Jubilation

KING GERARD
Free health checks for everyone by royal decree!

King Gerard and Queen Gerardine exit.

DOCTOR CHUFFLEBANGER

(To audience) Oh isn't that fabulous, free health checks for everybody. So lovely to see so many familiar faces here today. Richard, how's the rash? Have you told your wife yet? Just get her to rub it at night. Now I know one or two have been a little lax particularly you sir, so let's limber up. Get your gooses going. Goose goose, goose[7]. I grew up on a farm, you know. Worked with geese, goats, cows the three eared capawa[8]. Lonely job though, no-one to talk to, and I've always been a people person – so I said to my ma and pa the veterinary life's not for me, it's people I want to look after. So come on folks, time to get healthy. On your feet. *(She leads everyone in some silly circulation exercises)* That's it! Feel that rondos[9] running through your quenth[10]. Great that's wonderful. Now, who wants a free health check? Take advantage of our national health service while you still can!

Doctor Chufflebanger pulls up three audience members to the stage.

---

[7] Nasal haemorrhoids.

[8] The roaming headless beast of the Plains of Waa famous for running forwards and backwards at the same time without blinking. Feeds via osmosis so is keen on fish and chips but not in that order.

[9] Can either be like the Chinese concept of 'chi' or the French concept of 'ennui' depending on pollen count.

[10] Perfectly sized chuff nuts.

(To first audience member) Name please? *(First audience member states their name, Doctor Chufflebanger looks this up)* [name of audience member] Where are you from? Just touch your bishops for me would you. Excellent. Just going to check your cheff[11]? Wonderful. Just do this with your arm *(gives the first audience member a silly gesture to do then moves second audience member)* and I'll be right back. Name? *(Second audience member states their name, Doctor Chufflebanger looks this up)* Let's just have a listen to your flenge[12]? *(Puts stethoscope to audience member's knee and we hear strange voices)*. Ha! Multiple knee personality. Very common this time of year. Nothing to worry about. *(To third audience member)* Name? *(Third audience member states their name, Doctor Chufflebanger looks this up)* I see [name of audience member] Now let me just check your sem-sems[13]. *(She taps a hammer on first audience member's shoulder and we hear a sound effect)* Lovely. You'll be fine. *(To third audience member)* Excellent. Continue this daily and I'll see you in two weeks.

---

11 A romantic yet belligerent meeting between bacteria in which DNA and naughty stuff is transferred. See Vicky Wilson, molecular stylist to the stars, for more details.

12 Stripped fallopian tubes.

13 Under sized chuff nuts.

SCENE 2

A Market in Gwafalth

Dobson enters wheeling a cart filled with colourful, curious bottles and tins of all shapes and sizes. A sign displaying 'The Great Gazoombees' is mounted on the cart.

DOBSON

Roll up, roll up! Oh yes he's the man with the potions, the lotions and the motions. He'll cure your ailments, he'll fulfil your dreams and he'll dibble your dobsons. He's the one, he's the only… The Great Gazoombees.

The Great Gazoombees enters. He is a well-travelled, charming rogue. At various times throughout the song, The Great Gazoombees will perform sleight of hand tricks or fiery illusions as they sell various goods to customers.

SONG 2: THE GREAT GAZOOMBEES

DOBSON

See 'The Great Gazoombees'
And better your life
Take away pain
Take away strife
See 'The Great Gazoombees'
And better your life
He's the only man to do it for you

THE GREAT GAZOOMBEES
If your knees aching
If your fever's baking
If your skin is flaking
There's a little cure here for you

Sold that to a royal
She was awfully loyal
Cured her nasty boil
Never watered down one percent
I prefer to think of it as watered up

DOBSON & THE GREAT GAZOOMBEES
See 'The Great Gazoombees'
And better your life
Take away pain
Take away strife
See 'The Great Gazoombees'
And better your life
He's the only man to do it for you

THE GREAT GAZOOMBEES
If you're needing tooth floss
Suffering from hair loss
Wanna knock your boss off
Got a little rub here for you

Wanna change emotion
Try an ancient potion
Some exotic lotion

All free for the taking to you
As long as you can afford the price

DOBSON & THE GREAT GAZOOMBEES
See 'The Great Gazoombees'
And better your life
Take away pain
Take away strife
See 'The Great Gazoombees'
And better your life
He's the only man to do it for you

THE GREAT GAZOOMBEES
Something for the weekend
Following the new trend
Go on have a big spend
Guaranteed to work within days
by which time we'll be long gone

DOBSON & THE GREAT GAZOOMBEES
See 'The Great Gazoombees'
And better your life
Take away pain
Take away strife
See 'The Great Gazoombees'
And better your life
He's the only man to do
He's the only man to do
[Yes] He's the only man to do it for you

DOBSON

Side effects include diarrhoea, vomiting, death, more diarrhoea, more vomiting, more death, slow death, even slower death, basically tonnes of death, vomiting, diarrhoea and even more death. Terms and conditions apply. Always read the label.

THE GREAT GAZOOMBEES

Enough with the small print!

DOBSON

But aren't we're, like, legally bound to…

THE GREAT GAZOOMBEES

…I've never done nothin' legal in my life. *(To passers by)* Thank you folks, thank you. Nothing gives me more pleasure than taking good money from stupid people. *(To Dobson)* How did we do today? *(He flicks through a stack of notes)* Slim pickings. But, you did well, Dobson and fair is fair.

Having riffled through a few notes he hands him just one. He puts the rest of the money in his overcoat pocket and notices that it has split.

THE GREAT GAZOOMBEES

Finsbury Fumbles! Coat's got an hole in it. Stitch it, Dobson.

Dobson takes his coat and sits down to mend it. He feels a vial in the pocket.

DOBSON

What's this one, boss?

THE GREAT GAZOOMBEES

(Snatches) Eh, give that here.

DOBSON

But I thought none of these actually work?

THE GREAT GAZOOMBEES

Some of them does and some of them don't. And you my little quenbeth[14], will never know.

DOBSON

Oh please!

THE GREAT GAZOOMBEES

You really wanna know?

DOBSON

Yeah!

---

14 The mucky back department of the three eared Capawa.

THE GREAT GAZOOMBEES

It's delectable. Hint of strawberry, a trace of qualop[15] and the essence of cawahlee-kujayjay[16]. It'll have you smiling from ear to toe. You want some?

DOBSON

I'd love some.

THE GREAT GAZOOMBEES

Are you sure?

DOBSON

Oh yeah!

THE GREAT GAZOOMBEES

Be my guest!

DOBSON

Thanks, boss!

Dobson tries it.

DOBSON

I can't taste the strawberry, but perhaps a hint of qualop?

THE GREAT GAZOOMBEES

What about the essence of cawahlee-kujayjay?

---

[15] Ice cream without the cream and very little ice

[16] An inflatable fruit

DOBSON

Nah.

THE GREAT GAZOOMBEES

Oh Dobson! When are you gonna learn!

DOBSON

Learn what?

THE GREAT GAZOOMBEES

What do I do for a living?

DOBSON

Con man.

THE GREAT GAZOOMBEES

And what do con men do?

DOBSON

Lie. Ah right. This isn't going to end well for me is it?

THE GREAT GAZOOMBEES

No. *(Jiggling the bottle)* Dram-raks[17]!

DOBSON

What's going to happen?

---

17 Herbaceous poison as lethal as Janet Street Porter if taken in large doses.

THE GREAT GAZOOMBEES

Your legs gonna start to shake. Ooh there you go. *(Dobson starts to feel very ill as the symptoms emerge)* Brow a bit fevery. Mm? Feeling glandy, yeah yeah bit glandy? Head throbbing like a squalb[18]. Sudden cheff in your bishops, queasy in your mamflaps[19], And three, two, one…

Dobson drops to the ground in pain.

THE GREAT GAZOOMBEES

Very powerful poison that – and you've taken enough to flatten a whole herd of capawa. There's only one antidote – the Rapunzel herb - the rarest of the rare and I'm the only man who knows where it grows. Would you like some?

Dobson struggles to reach for the Rapunzel.

DOBSON

Rapunzel..!

THE GREAT GAZOOMBEES

Was that a yes?

DOBSON

Rapunzel..!

---

18 Gallic shrug with revolutionary tendencies.

19 A secretory marrow sized gland nestled behind your Dave Samsons.

THE GREAT GAZOOMBEES

Or a no?

DOBSON

Rapunzel..!

The Great Gazoombees toys with him, then finally gives him a taste of the herb.

DOBSON

Thank you.

THE GREAT GAZOOMBEES

And one, two three…

Dobson feels better and gets up.

THE GREAT GAZOOMBEES

Next time, I might not afford it to you. Right, next gig! *(He throws a newspaper at him)* What's out there?

DOBSON

Big delivery of marajujebs[20] coming in to the Nowenthian[21] docks.

---

[20] Hallucinogenic chestnuts.

[21] Relating to Nowen, a geographical anomaly. It only appears on non-foldable maps. The spiritual home of the towel. See Sleeping Beauty, Methuen, 2013.

THE GREAT GAZOOMBEES

Nah. Too risky.

DOBSON

Funeral of Barry the Fudge...

THE GREAT GAZOOMBEES

Funerals are good. But the Kazamarov twins[22] have got them sewn up. They're working out the East end now.

DOBSON

Masked ball in the Gazoobian mountains?

THE GREAT GAZOOMBEES

Hmm. Masked ball – we could do our lusty lord and his bawdy mistress routine.

DOBSON

No no please, not that...anything but that.

THE GREAT GAZOOMBEES

True you'd have to shave your gombles[23] – and I never wanna see them again. Not that close up! No we need something big, a real... gamer changer.

He keeps flicking through the paper.

---

22 Three halves of the recently defunct jazz infusion solo act 'Pencilectomy'.

23 Any citrus based combustible flan.

DOBSON

Oh wow!

THE GREAT GAZOOMBEES

Yes?

DOBSON

Four page spread on the King and Queen of Püss Püss – I love the royals.

THE GREAT GAZOOMBEES

The Royals! You lump of steaming smedge[24]. Think.

DOBSON

Strange. The King and Queen have got no hair.

THE GREAT GAZOOMBEES

What?

DOBSON

Says so here. No hair. Imagine that. Bald. Bald as a coot – both of them.

THE GREAT GAZOOMBEES

Let me see that. (*snatches the paper*) No, you lemsip. It's not that they've got no hair but that they've got no heir.

---

24 Laminated earwigs.

DOBSON

What?

THE GREAT GAZOOMBEES

It's not that they've got no hair but that they've got no heir.

DOBSON

Yeah. I know. No hair.

THE GREAT GAZOOMBEES

Not hair – heir!

DOBSON

I said that!

THE GREAT GAZOOMBEES

No. Hair, H.A.I.R is what's on your head. Heir, H.E.I.R – means a son or daughter to take over the kingdom.

DOBSON

Oh right.

THE GREAT GAZOOMBEES

Holy bandy bishops. Your quite staggering levels of stupidity have just given me an inspired idea.

DOBSON

Oh thanks boss.

THE GREAT GAZOOMBEES

(Pointing to himself) An heir! A prince. A King! There's only one man for the job.

DOBSON

You mean?

THE GREAT GAZOOMBEES

My finest creation.

DOBSON

The Baron Quell…

THE GREAT GAZOOMBEES

…son of Teth…

DOBSON

And second cousin of Randolph the Benge. But you haven't used him since…

THE GREAT GAZOOMBEES

(Violently silencing him)…Arsène Wenger.[25]!

DOBSON

Oh yeah.

---

[25] A physiological 'fight or flight' mechanism often resulting in wayward arm thrusts but of gargantuan therapeutic value.

THE GREAT GAZOOMBEES

This is my way out. All the other cons have been for money. But this, this is for a title.

DOBSON

What do you mean?

THE GREAT GAZOOMBEES

And with a title I'll never have to work again.

DOBSON

We'll...

THE GREAT GAZOOMBEES

Uh?

DOBSON

We'll...

THE GREAT GAZOOMBEES

We'll what?

DOBSON

We'll never have to work again.

THE GREAT GAZOOMBEES

Oh yeah, yeah 'we'll', obviously.

At various points throughout the song, The Great Gazoombees will perform sleight of hand tricks or fiery illusions.

THE GREAT GAZOOMBEES [REPRISE]

THE GREAT GAZOOMBEES
I will be the baron

DOBSON
I will be

THE GREAT GAZOOMBEES
my servant
Royals love a baron
If he's very travelled

DOBSON
And posh

THE GREAT GAZOOMBEES
Stories to amaze them

DOBSON
Little ways to praise them

THE GREAT GAZOOMBEES
Elevate and raise them
Unto heights of new

DOBSON
Joy!

THE GREAT GAZOOMBEES [Spoken]
Good Dobo!

THE GREAT GAZOOMBEES
Farewell to the old rags

DOBSON [Spoken]
Yeah!

THE GREAT GAZOOMBEES
[Yeah] You can carry my bags
Staying at the palace
While I'm gaining all of their trust

DOBSON [Spoken]
Then what?...

The Great Gazoombees laughs...

THE GREAT GAZOOMBEES
Soon 'The Great Gazoombees'
Will play his best game
With a new name
Seizing the reign...

THE GREAT GAZOOMBEES [Spoken]
You see what I did there, Dobson? Rein, R.E.I.N, is what you hold on to when riding a horse. But reign, R.E.I.G.N, is the rule of a King and Queen.

DOBSON [Spoken]
(Confused) I thought that was R.A.I.N?

THE GREAT GAZOOMBEES [Spoken]
No, no. R.A.I.N is this.

The Great Gazoombees picks up a small watering can and sprinkles water on to Dobson's head.

A long pause.

DOBSON [Spoken]
Oh yeah.

THE GREAT GAZOOMBEES
Then 'The Great Gazoombees'
Will rule the whole land
Never never never working again!

SCENE 3
The Gates of the Capitol

A sign saying 'Quarantine', Doctor Chufflebanger with a clipboard. King Gerard enters dressed in sporting apparel, carrying some sort of bat.

KING GERARD
Morning, Chuffers!

DOCTOR CHUFFLEBANGER
Sire, are you sure you should be down here?

KING GERARD
Well, yes, just come down to see how my old mucker Chuffers is getting on. Besides this pregnancy malarky, one can't do right for wrong. Ridiculous cravings at all hours, hormones all over the place. So I thought I'd sling the old, uh, johnson[26]... yes, yes, just having a bit of a stroll, you know, take the airs. *(Looking at the window)* Golly gonstables[27]. There must be a thousand people out there!

DOCTOR CHUFFLEBANGER
Yes Sire. So please move away from the window.

---

26 100% Egyptian polyester retractable hot pants.
27 Stiff capawa giblets.

KING GERARD

Windows eh! Yes, yes. Window. Love a window. I walked past one the other day, massive pane of glass. Totally clear. Hard but clear. Yes. Hmm. *(Seeing people at the window)* What are they all doing?

DOCTOR CHUFFLEBANGER

They're here to give their Shentel to you both.

KING GERARD

How charming. Shentel. *(Pensive)* Yes... yes...

DOCTOR CHUFFLEBANGER

I've tightened the restrictions to ensure no infection gets near the Queen at this delicate time in her pregnancy. So quarantine is rather overloaded at the moment.

KING GERARD

Jolly podkins[28], Chuffers. You're a good egg. *(Beat)* I don't suppose you'd be up for a game of riggeddy ding dong[29] this afternoon? No. No. Of course not. Always good to have a little break though. But you've got to get on. Lots of thing to do. Lots of things to do. Maybe a couple of quick sets? No. no, you're far too busy. Shame I've been working on a

---

28 Usually followed by the question "can you feel my moonpips?" - but not here.

29 A bit like underwater golf but with less supportive underwear.

new quap[30] - all from the elbow apparently. Got this new coach you see... marvellous chap, strange name though, foreign I think, never know how to pronounce it, don't want to ask, do you? Yes, yes... Anyway. Yes. Good, good. Things to do. Carry on... *(He exits)*

DOCTOR CHUFFLEBANGER

(Walks to the other door) Four nine five. Four nine five?

Dobson enters.

DOBSON

May I introduce...

DOCTOR CHUFFLEBANGER

Oh sorry, are you four nine five?

DOBSON

Oh, yes. May I introduce the Baron...

DOCTOR CHUFFLEBANGER

Oh a Baron! Yes. But have you got your ticket?

DOBSON

Yes I have! *(Hands his ticket over)*

---

30 A modern parlance a better version of an under-par lance.

DOCTOR CHUFFLEBANGER
Go on then!

DOBSON
The Baron Quell, son of Teth, second cousin of Randolph the Benge.

The Great Gazoombees enters. A flourish. NB: Where the text indicates [as Baron] after his name, The Great Gazoombees will put on an accent. Where this is not specifically indicated, The Great Gazoombees will speak in his normal voice.

THE GREAT GAZOOMBEES [as Baron]
(With great flair) Hemmmmm-u-shn[31]!

DOCTOR CHUFFLEBANGER
Ooh, that was fabulous, and what a wonderful coat. An exquisite example of Pilipostian haberdashery.

THE GREAT GAZOOMBEES [as Baron]
I am indeed from Pilipots; the spiritual home of the…

DOCTOR CHUFFLEBANGER
…flannel!

THE GREAT GAZOOMBEES [as Baron]
Ah a fellow flanneler!

---

[31] A silly noise

DOCTOR CHUFFLEBANGER
Ooh I love flannels.

THE GREAT GAZOOMBEES [as Baron]
Then maybe one day you will come to my village?

DOCTOR CHUFFLEBANGER
Woolwich?

THE GREAT GAZOOMBEES [as Baron]
Village. And we will spend the entire weekend flannelling to our hearts' content.

DOCTOR CHUFFLEBANGER
All weekend? I've never flannelled all weekend.

THE GREAT GAZOOMBEES [as Baron]
Then you haven't lived my cherub. I'll polish your bensons till they glisten like the brightest stars in the firmament, I'll shine your pom poms till they bedazzle all mankind. And as for what I'll do to your bouncy bebs, you'll just have to wait and see.

DOCTOR CHUFFLEBANGER
Ooh I say! (*Composing herself*) Right if I may just, ask for your papers.

THE GREAT GAZOOMBEES [as Baron]
Of course, my angel.

DOCTOR CHUFFLEBANGER

(Perusing the papers) Mm hmm... This seems.. Ah hah... Right... Mm... *(Puts the papers down, to Baron)* Cover your left phelp[32]...

The Great Gazoombees puts a hand over his left eye.

DOCTOR CHUFFLEBANGER

...and read the chart with your elbow.

THE GREAT GAZOOMBEES [as Baron]

(Reading the chart with ridiculously noises, which can be the same or totally different to each other[33]) Gr. Sh. Fffff. Ng. gee. *! Shurp. Téng. Ba ^^ rG.

DOCTOR CHUFFLEBANGER

Excellent. Twenty twenty! Can you hear this? *(No sound is heard)*

THE GREAT GAZOOMBEES [as Baron]

Yes.

DOCTOR CHUFFLEBANGER

And this? *(No sound is heard)*

---

32 Similar to a strapless cupless brazier. May cause indigestion.

33 These represent the sonic, phonetic, hassidic and often alkaline letters of the Püss Püssian alphabet.

THE GREAT GAZOOMBEES [as Baron]
(Putting their hands to the ears as if it's loud) Ooh yeah!

DOCTOR CHUFFLEBANGER
And this? *(He makes a loud, silly sound)*

THE GREAT GAZOOMBEES [as Baron]
Nope.

DOCTOR CHUFFLEBANGER
Great. And you. Think of a mongoose.

He does.

DOCTOR CHUFFLEBANGER
Perfect. Now walk like a capawa.

He does impression of the bird with noises. Doctor Chufflebanger now conducts a physical examination.

DOCTOR CHUFFLEBANGER
Lovely. *(She squirts them both with antibacterial spray)* That's you done. So exciting isn't it – the Queen's pregnancy!

THE GREAT GAZOOMBEES [as Baron]
The what?

DOCTOR CHUFFLEBANGER

Pregnancy. Just happened last week. I assumed that's why you were here?

THE GREAT GAZOOMBEES [as Baron]

Ah…err..?

DOCTOR CHUFFLEBANGER

To give your Shentel?

THE GREAT GAZOOMBEES [as Baron]

Oh yes of course… of course. *(To himself)* Oh Finsbury fumbles, and double deng on toast!

DOCTOR CHUFFLEBANGER

What was that?

THE GREAT GAZOOMBEES [as Baron]

I said neegronsky fredykov [34], hamal humpsteed [35] and Gaaaree Linekoo[36].

DOCTOR CHUFFLEBANGER

Gaaaree Linekoo?

---

[34] A defamatory phrase nearly as rude as Jonny's saucepan.

[35] A possible reference to any Hertfordshire based new town but highly and lowly unlikely.

[36] Pertaining or not pertaining to national treasures.

THE GREAT GAZOOMBEES [as Baron]
June Invaaadal and Clare Booouuulding.[37].

DOCTOR CHUFFLEBANGER
It certainly didn't sound like you said that.

THE GREAT GAZOOMBEES [as Baron]
Then maybe it is you, dear Doctor, who needs an earring toast.

Doctor Chufflebanger looks at The Great Gazoombees suspiciously as he makes to leave.

DOCTOR CHUFFLEBANGER
Maybe. (*suddenly plays the coy mistress*) Just one moment. A final touch of the flannel before you go?

THE GREAT GAZOOMBEES [as Baron]
Of course.

DOCTOR CHUFFLEBANGER
The weave, the weft, the nap - astonishing. The fabric so fine yet so sturdy? It's amazing. *(She pricks him with a small implement)*

THE GREAT GAZOOMBEES [as Baron]
What was that?

---

[37] See 36.

DOCTOR CHUFFLEBANGER
Sorry…over excited. You're free from infection – enjoy your time in the court.

They exit.

DOCTOR CHUFFLEBANGER
(She holds up the implement now complete with blood sample) Hmm, let's get Geoff at the lab has to test this. There's something fishy about the those two. *(She picks up a large plastic fish and speaks into it)* Geoff? Chuffers here…

SCENE 4

The Royal Palace

FAIRY 1 (V/O)

Certainly didn't take long for The Great Gazoombees aka 'the baron' to gain the confidence of the King and Queen.

FAIRY 2 (V/O)

But let's just hope the noble Doctor can see through his evil plot.

The Great Gazoombees stands in an alpha male position, engrossing everyone in his story. King Gerard and Queen Gerardine hang on every word.

THE GREAT GAZOOMBEES [as Baron]

...so I did what any red-blooded man would do. I grabbed his hanging Jacksons[38] and squeezed and squeezed until they popped. Pop. Pop. Pop. Yes he had three hanging Jacksons. Who knew!

Queen Gerardine and The Great Gazoombees burst into laughter. King Gerard feels the pain of the imagined squeeze before joining in.

THE GREAT GAZOOMBEES [as Baron]

...and after that the whole village was saved and Kingdom prospered once more.

---

38 Sensitive glands just being your Hunniford pipe.

KING GERARD
Ah Baron, you deserve far more praise for these tasks.

THE GREAT GAZOOMBEES [as Baron]
No it not just me, it was mainly me, but also other people, there were no other people, I mustn't take all the credit, although most would but humility is next to virility.

QUEEN GERARDINE
(Coy) Ooh, you're certainly full of that Baron!

THE GREAT GAZOOMBEES [as Baron]
Graaa!

They burst into laughter again.

THE GREAT GAZOOMBEES [as Baron]
Your highness, your beauty is unfathomable. *(He kisses her hand in an elaborate way)* It reminds me of the tale of the humble dancing shepherd and his manically depressed yak.

QUEEN GERARDINE
Oh, we don't know that one.

THE GREAT GAZOOMBEES [as Baron]
First we meet the humble dancing Shepherd. *(He performs the short introductory dance of the shepherd, accompanied by sound effects)* Now we meet the manically depressed yak. *(He performs the short introductory dance of the yak, accompanied by sound effects)* But the shepherd has forgotten

his flowers. *(Beat)* Yes, I know, the ending is a little weak. Where are the flowers, one wonders? *(Suddenly with a massive guttural sound he produces as bunch of flowers from thin air.)*

QUEEN GERARDINE
(Startled and excited) Oh!

THE GREAT GAZOOMBEES [as Baron]
And you, your majesty. What a face you have. *(He takes his face in his hands and massages it seductively, the King is nervous but likes it)* What noble nose, what regal cheeks, what astonishing thighs.

KING GERARD
Ooh I say!

THE GREAT GAZOOMBEES [as Baron]
I bet a man such as you doesn't care for rules and conventions. No, you are a man who walks to the beat of his own drum. Rum pa-pa-pum. Rum pa-pa-pum. Rum pa-pa-pum...

King Gerard joins in.

KING GERARD & THE GREAT GAZOOMBEES [as Baron]
Rum pa-pa-pum. Rum pa-pa-pum. Rum pa-pa-pum...

THE GREAT GAZOOMBEES [as Baron]
(Loudly) Pum!

KING GERARD
(Jumps) Oh!

THE GREAT GAZOOMBEES [as Baron]
Your majesties, I have overstayed my welcome. I must take my leave.

QUEEN GERARDINE
Absolutely not. It feels like you've only just arrived.

KING GERARD
Here, here. Won't you stay for a few more weeks, old chap?

QUEEN GERARDINE
Baron. *(Flirting)* Your Queen insists.

KING GERARD
As does your King.

THE GREAT GAZOOMBEES [as Baron]
I'm deeply humbled and touched by your unparalleled generosity.

QUEEN GERARDINE
Then that's settled.

THE GREAT GAZOOMBEES [as Baron]
But I can only accept this gift of hospitality if you accept my gift of libation. Allow me to pour you a glass, as is tradition in my country.

QUEEN GERARDINE
How delightful.

KING GERARD
But Gerardine, you know the rules.

King Gerard rings a bell.

QUEEN GERARDINE
Oh Gerard, must we always summon the Doctor for such trivial matters?

KING GERARD
It's for your health, Gerardine.

QUEEN GERARDINE
I'm fed up of everybody double checking my every move. Like the Baron says, it's time to walk to the beat of our own drum. Rum pa-pa-pum. Rum pa-pa-pum.

DOCTOR CHUFFLEBANGER
(Entering) Your majesties.

QUEEN GERARDINE
Doctor, I am having some wine.

DOCTOR CHUFFLEBANGER

Of course a small glass before bedtime will help settle the pem-pebs[39].

THE GREAT GAZOOMBEES [as Baron]

Allow me.

DOCTOR CHUFFLEBANGER

I'm afraid I must first examine all food and beverage.

QUEEN GERARDINE

Oh I 'm fed up of this. No heavy lifting, no eating blue cheese, no dying your hair, no sunbathing, all these restrictions just make me want to do more. I never even liked cats - but now I want one just so I can change the litter. I just want to be normal. I can't remember the last time I even chewed on a neb neb[40].

THE GREAT GAZOOMBEES [as Baron]

(To King Gerard) Your majesty?

KING GERARD

We can decide who pours our wine thank you, Doctor.

---

39 A gargantuan bedpan that threateneth to overfloweth.

40 Juicy biscuits.

DOCTOR CHUFFLEBANGER

(To King Gerard) But, Sire, this is Haile Selassie[41]!

QUEEN GERARDINE

Nonsense. Doctor, doctor, relax. Have the afternoon off.

DOCTOR CHUFFLEBANGER

But... but...

KING GERARD

Leave us!

Doctor Chufflebanger exits.

THE GREAT GAZOOMBEES [as Baron]

Shall I be Mum?

KING GERARD

Absolutely. Now... not that Babuüsian[42] plonk *(exiting and returning with a bottle)* try this, been saving it for a special occasion.

He hands it to The Great Gazoombees who opens it and pours three glasses.

---

41 Mother, son and latter day accountant of the former Emperor of Ethiopia.

42 Relating to Babuüs, the industrial core of Waa but without the pips .The spiritual home of the quilt. See Sleeping Beauty, Methuen, 2013.

QUEEN GERARDINE

And fetch the Ferrero Rocher, Gerard!

KING GERARD

The Ferrero Rocher from the Ambassador's receptions that are noted for their exquisite taste.

QUEEN GERARDINE

Yes. Why not!

THE GREAT GAZOOMBEES [as Baron]

What is this Ferrero Rocher?

QUEEN GERARDINE

Ferrero Rocher!

KING GERARD

Ferrero Rocher.

QUEEN GERARDINE

Try one!

They all do, in turn remarking on the taste.

KING GERARD

Mm. Fnezg[43]!

---

43 Phonetic variation of the word 'dentist'.

QUEEN GERARDINE
Mm. Shnayblee[44].

THE GREAT GAZOOMBEES [as Baron]
Mm. Doooooooooooooh[45]!

They all turn to the audience and sing in harmony.

KING GERARD & QUEEN GERARDINE & THE GREAT GAZOOMBEES [as Baron]
[Singing] Ferrero Rocher!

He hands out the glasses. He sniffs his glass.

THE GREAT GAZOOMBEES [as Baron]
Oh this is wonderful. But to appreciate a grape of such depth, we must close our assesh!

KING GERARD
Our what?

THE GREAT GAZOOMBEES [as Baron]
(Indicating his eyes) Our assesh.

KING GERARD
Ooooh. Our eyes! Eyes yes. That's a relief.

---

44 Phonetic variation of the word 'dentist'.
45 Phonetic variation of the word 'dentist'.

THE GREAT GAZOOMBEES [as Baron]
Why what did you think I said?

KING GERARD
Oh... oh... no no, I... er, quite.

They all close their eyes. The Great Gazoombees instantly opens his. He loudly sniffs the wine. They follow suit and he places some herbs into Queen Gerardine's glass. They open their eyes and raise their glasses.

THE GREAT GAZOOMBEES [as Baron]
Shniiiiiiiizg[46]!

KING GERARD & QUEEN GERARDINE & THE GREAT GAZOOMBEES [as Baron]
Shniiiiiiiizg!

King Gerard and The Greet Gazoombees drink, Queen Gerardine is too concerned with the Ferrero Rocher.

THE GREAT GAZOOMBEES [as Baron]
(Coaxing Queen Gerardine to drink) Do know what Shniiiiiiiizg is it in my language?

---

[46] Literally 'May your shelving units become prone to depression!'

QUEEN GERARDINE
No!

THE GREAT GAZOOMBEES [as Baron]
Noodi, roodi, noodi roodi pop chops[47].

QUEEN GERARDINE
Oh I love that!

KING GERARD & QUEEN GERARDINE & THE GREAT GAZOOMBEES [as Baron]
(Raising their glasses) Noodi, roodi, noodi roodi pop chops.

They all drink.

KING GERARD
Good quaff, eh. Quaffable isn't it. Very quaffable.

THE GREAT GAZOOMBEES
Three, two, one…

QUEEN GERARDINE
Yes yes… quaffable. *(She hiccups)* Oops, the lady doth quaff too much, methinks. Oh dear *(feeling queasy)* I'm feeling rather… *(puts her hand on her stomach)*

---

47 The exact moment a petite pois metamorphoses into a grande pois.

THE GREAT GAZOOMBEES [as Baron]
Too many Ferrero Rochers?

QUEEN GERARDINE
Probably Baron yes.

KING GERARD
This happened at the ambassador's party.

THE GREAT GAZOOMBEES [as Baron]
What the ambassador's party known for its exquisite taste?

KING GERARD
Yes! *(To Queen Gerardine)* Darling? *(To The Great Gazoombees)* Maybe it's best we retired.

THE GREAT GAZOOMBEES [as Baron]
(Aside) Apt choice of words! *(To King Gerard and Queen Gerardine)* Of course. I pray you will feel better in the morning... *(as they have exited)* but I doubt it.

They exit. The two fairy puppets appear.

FAIRY 1 (V/O)
The Queen of course starting to feel the very early affects of the Dram-raks. So small and yet... so potent.

FAIRY 2 (V/O)

The days and weeks move on – and the baron administers more and more of the poisonous potion and the Queen grows sicker and sicker.

[Continues…]

SCENE 5
The Royal Palace

King Gerard, The Great Gazoombees and Dobson sit waiting in nervous anticipation. Centre stage, a door is prominently lit.

[...Continued]

FAIRY 1 (V/O)
And now, with all medical methods thus far failed, the noble Doctor tries one last treatment to save the Queen and her unborn child. We remember of course only a few months ago, Fairy John, we were here celebrating with such great joy.

FAIRY 2 (V/O)
It's hard to remain impartial at times like this but our hearts go out to the King and Queen of Püss Püss.

FAIRY 1 (V/O)
And the kingdom is hushed in anticipation of the prognosis.

The door opens and Doctor Chufflebanger emerges.

KING GERARD
Doctor?

During the song, The Great Gazoombees and Dobson console King Gerard.

SONG 3: MALADY

DOCTOR CHUFFLEBANGER

I have never seen
Such a malady before
I have tried and fought
But I fear there's nothing more
This disease inside
It is nothing I have known
There is something very strange
And it chills me to the bone

KING GERARD

But she lives?

DOCTOR CHUFFLEBANGER

Though the Queen still breathes
now her body cannot mend
As the seasons change
She may never rise again
For her eyes are glazed
and the fever's in her brain

KING GERARD

What, the fever's in the brain?

DOCTOR CHUFFLEBANGER

She can barely say her name…

KING GERARD

But our baby, our heir, our one and only
To be born from out of all this strife
Such a dark dark day should be filled with so much joy
not the questions of death over life

DOCTOR CHUFFLEBANGER

Though her heart is strong
There is nothing we can do
Though the day is long
It is clear she'll not pull through
We will loose her soon
We will loose her and the child

KING GERARD

What the mother *and* the child?

ALL

Both the mother and the child

KING GERARD

Is there no cure, Doctor?

DOCTOR CHUFFLEBANGER / GREAT GAZOOMBEES / DOBSON

If I knew from whence all this malady derived
Feeling joyous, feeling happy
Then a cure might be within sight
It seems my plan is working

It defies all science, neither features on my shelf and soon the kingdom will be mine
I have failed you, my liege, this night

THE GREAT GAZOOMBEES [Spoken]
You see Dobo. What do con men do?

DOBSON [Spoken]
Lie.

THE GREAT GAZOOMBEES [Spoken]
Lie... *(Sung)* Ah ah ah...

DOCTOR CHUFFLEBANGER
Now her life does wane
There is nothing more to say
I shall ease her pain
I shall help, Sir, each day

KING GERARD
Can you say how long?

DOCTOR CHUFFLEBANGER
I simply cannot say
I shall take my leave.

DOCTOR CHUFFLEBANGER [Spoken]
Your majesty. I'm sorry. *(She exits)*

KING GERARD
If only there was something.

THE GREAT GAZOOMBEES [as Baron]
I suppose when all known medicine has failed...

KING GERARD
Yes?

THE GREAT GAZOOMBEES [as Baron]
We turn to... alternative measures.

KING GERARD
Metric?

THE GREAT GAZOOMBEES [as Baron]
No. Not all medicine comes from book. I've heard of a witch who grows a herb so powerful it will cure any ailment.

KING GERARD
Any ailment?

THE GREAT GAZOOMBEES [as Baron]
The Rapunzel herb.

KING GERARD
The Rapunzel herb?

THE GREAT GAZOOMBEES [as Baron]
But it comes with a heavy price.

KING GERARD
Money's no object.

THE GREAT GAZOOMBEES [as Baron]
It's never money.

KING GERARD
What then?

THE GREAT GAZOOMBEES [as Baron]
Phff. A curse? A sacrifice? One time a miniature but quite useful stationary set; pencil sharpener, compass, protractor, another time dinner with Gloria Hunniford. She's crazy. I could not live with myself to broker such a deal for you.

KING GERARD
But what price worse than loosing them both! Do it – whatever it takes, and whatever happens you will never be to blame, my good friend.

THE GREAT GAZOOMBEES [as Baron]
I am ever your humble servant.

SCENE 6
The Woods

Dobson is alone, the cart is on stage, he has a basket beside him.

DOBSON
Right, that's the handkerchiefs washed. Time to dry 'em. I've done most of 'em. A con man's assistant's work is never done. Particularly with The Great Gazoombees. I know he's a mean 'un, but he's all I got. Sometimes it would be lovely to have a helping hand. Shame there's no-one about.

He rustles around in the cart and produces a length of rope. What follows is a version of the magic trick 'The Magic Washing Line'. He goes into the wings and ties off one end. He crosses the stage into the opposite wing and ties off the other end. He returns and looks around. He spots a member of the audience.

DOBSON
Oh hello humble woodsman! What's your name? Are you busy? Would you mind helping me. *(He brings an audience member up on stage)* Just need to hang these hankies up. Thank you so much. *(He passes them the basket)* Now if hold this, I'll tie these up. They're not going to fall off are they? *(The audience member confirms)* No, no. Nice and tight. Great. Right, that's all done. Thank you so much. *(He ushers the audience member back to their seat)* Couldn't have done it without you. Bravo!

He stands back and looks proudly at the washing line.

DOBSON

Oh no. There's no wind. Take ages to dry. *(Has an idea, approaches the audience member who had helped)* I think I'm going to need your help again. *(He sees more of the audience)* Subsequent humble woodsman... *(Seeing the rest of the audience)* Subsequent subsequent humble woodsfolk! Can you help me dry the hankies? Can you all help me to generate some wind. Not that kind of wind! Like this *(He does a sound and a gesture)*. Ready? One, two three. *(The audience blow and the handkerchiefs start to flutter)* It's working! More wind. *(The handkerchiefs start shaking)* More wind. *(They shake more)*

Suddenly all the handkerchiefs drop to the ground, their knots in tact and the line still tight.

DOBSON

Too much wind! Oh no...

The Great Gazoombees enters.

THE GREAT GAZOOMBEES

Oi, what are them hankies doing on the floor!

DOBSON

Sorry boss, they're definitely dry now. *(Collecting them up)* We can venture forth!

THE GREAT GAZOOMBEES
Venture what?

DOBSON
Venture forth on our perilous quest to find the witch!

THE GREAT GAZOOMBEES
Oh not again. What do I do for a living?

DOBSON
Con man?

THE GREAT GAZOOMBEES
What do con men do every day?

DOBSON
Co… Oh, I see! It was all a lie. There is no witch.

THE GREAT GAZOOMBEES
Of course not, you lemsip.

DOBSON
So we going back to the palace then?

THE GREAT GAZOOMBEES
No! It's all about timing. Go back now, sure – be a hero. But wait 'til they're really desperate and they're ain't nothing they won't do.

DOBSON

What is it you want them to do?

THE GREAT GAZOOMBEES

To make me heir!

DOBSON

But you've already got hair.

THE GREAT GAZOOMBEES

Stop splitting hairs. Patience my boy. The best cons are the long cons!

DOBSON

Chutney Bishops[48], you're good. The King and Queen love you.

THE GREAT GAZOOMBEES

Love? Hmm. Well...

DOBSON

Has there ever been a love in your life?

THE GREAT GAZOOMBEES

Don't!

DOBSON

Who was...?

---

[48] A curiously pleasant bout of deep sea thrombosis.

THE GREAT GAZOOMBEES

(Violently silencing him)...Arsène Venger! *(Beat)* No. It's time I spoke out.

DOBSON

So. Who was she?

THE GREAT GAZOOMBEES

She? *(Pause)* He?

DOBSON

He?

THE GREAT GAZOOMBEES

He. *(Beat, he approaches the campfire)* Derek was just a little boy, and I was just a little boy. We were like three brothers, Derek and me. Life was simple. Maths was hard.

Blackout. Lights Up. The Great Gazoombees is mid flow. Dobson is tired and bored.

THE GREAT GAZOOMBEES

...which is really funny if you think about it. 'Cause mauve's not generally my colour.

Blackout. Lights Up. The Great Gazoombees is mid flow. Both have scruffy mid-size beards. Dobson, bored, twiddles his.

THE GREAT GAZOOMBEES

...it's his favourite song and all – ke so me lo kekekek gru pa[49].

Blackout. Lights Up. Both have massive beards. Dobson's has been shaped and waxed.

THE GREAT GAZOOMBEES

...then after I had my tonsils out, he never spoke to me again.

DOBSON

So how did you get to be a con man?

THE GREAT GAZOOMBEES

Now *that's* a *long* story. Come on. *(Getting up)* Get some mud and smear it on yourself.

DOBSON

Why?

THE GREAT GAZOOMBEES

'Cause it's gotta look like we've been travelling a most arduous journey for these past months, fraught with danger and peril. Where's your sense of drama!?

---

49 Lyrics from the love/hate ballad 'Unconscious Crumbling', a song about when married celebrity chefs separate but pretend to still like each other in public.

FAIRY 1 (V/O)
Back at the palace tragedy looks only moments away. The Queen's health deteriorates further.

FAIRY 2 (V/O)
It's been months since Gazoombees left – you and I know he's siting out there biding his time. But come on, it's gotta be a straight red card for this sort of behaviour.

FAIRY 1 (V/O)
This is unbearable.

SCENE 7
The Royal Palace

King Gerard sits beside the bed, distraught. Queen Gerardine lies, weary.

QUEEN GERARDINE
(Weakly) My King! My Gerard. I can fight no more.

KING GERARD
No, my love. You must hold on.

Dobson plays a sound effect of ethereal bliss as the doors fly open and he and The Great Gazoombees enter, exhausted, dehydrated, clothes ripped, hands bandaged, faces dirtied.

KING GERARD
He's returned my Queen. I knew he would.

THE GREAT GAZOOMBEES [as Baron]
I have it, sire. The Rapunzel herb.

KING GERARD
The Rapunzel herb. We're saved!

THE GREAT GAZOOMBEES [as Baron]
But… the price!

KING GERARD
The price?

THE GREAT GAZOOMBEES [as Baron]
Your child.

Queen Gerardine cries out in pain.

KING GERARD
What do you mean?

THE GREAT GAZOOMBEES [as Baron]
The witch, she will take your baby as her own.

KING GERARD
Our baby?

THE GREAT GAZOOMBEES [as Baron]
This is her price.

KING GERARD
Or else?

THE GREAT GAZOOMBEES [as Baron]
Or else…

He looks to Dobson to give him his cue. Dobson prepares to shake his thunder sheet.

THE GREAT GAZOOMBEES [as Baron]
…we shall all be cursed.

Thunder.

KING GERARD

If we don't do this, both mother and child will die. Give me the herb.

King Gerard approaches Queen Gerardine with the Rapunzel herb. Doctor Chufflebanger rushes on with a paper in her hand.

DOCTOR CHUFFLEBANGER

Sire! *(Seeing the herb)* What are you doing?

KING GERARD

Keep out of this.

DOCTOR CHUFFLEBANGER

Who gave you that? *(Indicating The Great Gazoombees)* This man?

KING GERARD

This will cure her, Doctor.

DOCTOR CHUFFLEBANGER

But sire this is Haile Selassie! You cannot believe anything he has told you.

KING GERARD

What are you talking about, Chuffers?

DOCTOR CHUFFLEBANGER
I have here the results of a blood test taken on the day of his arrival. The secretions of his honesty gland indicate a lifetime of deception.

KING GERARD
This man has risked his life for us.

Queen Gerardine cries out…

THE GREAT GAZOOMBEES [as Baron]
Your majesty, you must administer the herb.

King Gerard approaches the bed.

DOCTOR CHUFFLEBANGER
Whatever he's told you is a lie.

KING GERARD
Take this my love.

King Gerard gives Queen Gerardine the Rapunzel.

DOCTOR CHUFFLEBANGER
Don't do it, your majesty…

QUEEN GERARDINE
My body, my choice.

Queen Gerardine takes the herb. She coughs and splutters. It doesn't look good. Doctor Chufflebanger runs up to the Queen and takes her pulse.

DOCTOR CHUFFLEBANGER
I'm a doctor for heaven's sake.

KING GERARD
What's happening?

DOCTOR CHUFFLEBANGER
(Confused) Her pulse is getting stronger.

THE GREAT GAZOOMBEES [as Baron]
And the fever will ease.

Queen Gerardine starts to recover...

KING GERARD
My Queen?

THE GREAT GAZOOMBEES
And one... two... three...

QUEEN GERARDINE
I feel much... better... much much better Gerard.

THE GREAT GAZOOMBEES [as Baron]
It seems, Doctor Chufflebanger, that all is well.

KING GERARD
Leave us, Doctor. And thank you Baron.

SCENE 8
The Woods

The Great Gazoombees and Dobson are walking through the woods, laden with nappies, dummies, milk and other supplies for a newborn baby. At a crossroads The Great Gazoombees and Dobson go opposite directions.

DOBSON
Palace is this way.

THE GREAT GAZOOMBEES
Uh?

DOBSON
Palace is this way.

THE GREAT GAZOOMBEES
I know.

DOBSON
Then why are you going that way?

THE GREAT GAZOOMBEES
To dump the nappies in the tower.

DOBSON
The nappies for the new baby Rapunzel when she's born.

THE GREAT GAZOOMBEES
Yes.

DOBSON
But Rapunzel is going to be taken by the witch.

THE GREAT GAZOOMBEES
Have you forgotten already? It's exhausting with you!

DOBSON
Eh?

THE GREAT GAZOOMBEES
What do I do for a living?

DOBSON
Hang on, hang on, I remember this one. Con man?

THE GREAT GAZOOMBEES
What do con men do every day?

DOBSON
Wait wait wait… no don't tell me… Lie. Oh, yeah, there is no witch – and you're taking Rapunzel.

THE GREAT GAZOOMBEES
Genius.

DOBSON

You're taking Rapunzel and you're gonna slaughter her mercilessly.

THE GREAT GAZOOMBEES

That's right, Bovril, I'm going to kill her. That's why I've just bought a year's supply of nappies, powered milk and this tupperware breast pump. I'm a con man not a murderer.

DOBSON

I don't understand.

THE GREAT GAZOOMBEES

Dobson, there comes a certain time in everyone's life, when you gotta re-evaluate things. I'm gonna look after this baby – and with no other heir apparent, I will make sure that I am the only apparent heir. Ipso facto I will be King.

DOBSON

And I can be the Kings's favourite chamber maid… no chamberlain!

THE GREAT GAZOOMBEES

(Aside) Chamber pot more like!

DOBSON

Amazing. What a double act, we are, eh! What a team!

SONG 4: PARTNERS

We fit together like a hand in a glove
Working the room so sweet
You distract them and I win them with love
Yes we're a team complete

It's easier living when you're living as two
I miss you when you're gone
Be hard achieving all the things that we do
If we were only one

Partners, what it's all about
Partners, what a team
Partners we're the perfect pair
A partnershipping dream

I put the 'i' into a magical touch
You put the 'u' in fraud
Being alone I didn't like much
With you I'm never bored

What is a capawa with only two ears
It's like a flightless bird
What is a deck chair but without any decks
It's totally absurd

Partners, what it's all about
Partners, what a team
Partners we're the perfect pair
A partnershipping dream

Partners, what it's all about
Partners, what a team
Partners we're the perfect pair
A double-dipping, power-skipping, partnershipping dream

THE GREAT GAZOOMBEES
Right, now hop it. You're fired.

DOBSON
What?

THE GREAT GAZOOMBEES
Business mate. You're like a lead weight around my neck – and I'm not having you shent this one up.

SCENE 9
The Royal Palace

King Gerard and The Great Gazoombees are waiting in nervous anticipation. Centre stage, a door is prominently lit. Two fairy puppets appear.

FAIRY 1 (V/O)
Here we go again. The royal birth is upon us, tension once more…

We hear a baby crying. King Gerard stands.

DOCTOR CHUFFLEBANGER (V/O)
There it is. The sound of new life.

QUEEN GERARDINE (Offstage)
What is it?

DOCTOR CHUFFLEBANGER (Offstage)
It's a beautiful baby girl, your Majesty.

QUEEN GERARDINE (Offstage)
A girl! Let me hold her.

DOCTOR CHUFFLEBANGER (Offstage)
I'm sorry your Majesty.

QUEEN GERARDINE (Offstage)
Please!

DOCTOR CHUFFLEBANGER (Offstage)
I'm acting under Royal Decree.

QUEEN GERARDINE (Offstage)
Royal Decree? Royal Decree?!

Queen Gerardine bursts in.

QUEEN GERARDINE
Gerard, I want to hold my baby.

King Gerard indicates for Doctor Chufflebanger to fetch the baby.

KING GERARD
Maybe for a moment?

THE GREAT GAZOOMBEES [as Baron]
Your Highness, we do not have this moment of which you speak. The witch, she's outside in quite a small carriage with very large hamsters. She's arranged a baby shower at the new Halfords store with Gloria Hunniford.

KING GERARD
Thank you.

THE GREAT GAZOOMBEES [as Baron]
Clare Booouuulding.

Doctor Chufflebanger re-enters with the baby and hands it over to Queen Gerardine.

QUEEN GERARDINE
My sweet, sweet girl. I'm sorry, I thought this was meant to be. My sweet darling…Rapunzel.

She kisses the baby.

QUEEN GERARDINE
Now take her.

The Great Gazoombees takes the baby and exits.

QUEEN GERARDINE
I pray you will be loved.

THE GREAT GAZOOMBEES [as Baron]
Doctor.

DOCTOR CHUFFLEBANGER
This is your doing!

QUEEN GERARDINE
Leave me.

King Gerard approaches her.

QUEEN GERARDINE
Leave me!

Queen Gerardine is left alone on stage.

They exit. King Gerard lingers for a moment longer. They exchange a loving look. He leaves.

SONG 5: WE WERE MEANT TO BE...

QUEEN GERARDINE
One precious moment
Just you and me
And you were beautiful
Beautiful to see

So small so tender
Felt like I won
This perfect part of me
This part of me has gone

Yes we were meant to be together
All through the days and nights forever
Then some day you'll find me
Then some day you'll hold me

Playing in tree-tops
You'll sing and run
But who'll be there for you
When the day is done?

Over the last verse of the song, it begins to snow.

Skating with mummy
As the snow falls
Will be with someone else
Someone who's not yours

Yes we were meant to be together
Just you and me for all for ever
Some day I will find you
Some day I will hold you…

King Gerard enters.

QUEEN GERARDINE & KING GERARD
Though we are meant to be together / She'll have her mother's heart
Just you and me for all for ever / Her strength and grace
Some day I will find you / Her wit and charm
Some day I will hold you / Her noble face

Though we are meant to be together / She'll have her mother's eyes
Just you and me for all for ever / That look so rare
Some day I will find you / Her warmth and grace
Some day I will hold you / Such flowing hair

QUEEN GERARDINE
Be good to others
As you expect them to be
But if you call my name…
[Spoken] Oh, Gerard.

He opens up his arms. They walk off in an embrace. Doctor Chufflebanger enters from another part of the stage.

DOCTOR CHUFFLEBANGER

(Holding a large plastic fish to her ear) Saddle the capawa. Give me your best twelve riders. We leave at once.

ACT TWO
PROLOGUE

A puff of smoke and two fairy puppets appear.

FAIRY 1 (V/O)
Well the audience starting to settle back into their seats, as is their wont.

FAIRY 2 (V/O)
Seeing some of the sweeties on display, Fairy John, I'm certainly feeling a little peckish myself.

FAIRY 1 (V/O)
Ferrero Rocher?

FAIRY 2 (V/O)
From the ambassador's reception?

FAIRY 1 (V/O)
The ambassador of course known for his exquisite taste.

Sports theme sound effect.

FAIRY 1 (V/O)
Well, back after half time of course, and so much has happened.

FAIRY 2 (V/O)

Eighteen years is a long time. Even for the most experienced of players.

FAIRY 1 (V/O)

Under the pressure of insurmountable grief, the Royals decided to find the witch and plead for Rapunzel's safe return.

FAIRY 2 (V/O)

But the witch purely a figment of the evil Baron's imagination, was nowhere to be found.

FAIRY 1 (V/O)

And after years without success, the grief became too much for our noble Queen who so tragically passed away.

[Continues…]

SCENE 1
The Royal Palace

[...Continued]

FAIRY 2 (V/O)
So here we are on the day of the 18th annual search party that has come to commemorate Rapunzel's birth.

FAIRY 1 (V/O)
We rejoin as the King prepares to serve.

The Great Gazoombees enters.

KING GERARD
What news?

THE GREAT GAZOOMBEES [as Baron]
Nothing, Sire. Rapunzel was nowhere to be found.

KING GERARD
A dark cloak descends upon this Kingdom.

THE GREAT GAZOOMBEES [as Baron]
Alack the day.

KING GERARD
(Mournfully) Aled Jones... yes. First dear Rapunzel, and then my Queen.

THE GREAT GAZOOMBEES [as Baron]
A father's hope should never die.

KING GERARD
A father? I've never really felt much like a father…

THE GREAT GAZOOMBEES [as Baron]
I leave… while you sing song.

The Great Gazoombees exits.

SONG 6: HOW CAN I BE YOURS

KING GERARD
How can I be yours
When you're with another
I seek a little sunshine round my door
But now I'm afraid if I should seek it any more

And I see you there
Close enough to hold me
And I need you here
Wrap me in your arms
But I'm scared for you
I don't know the journey that you're going on

Maybe I'll be yours
We could be together
Maybe you'll be frightened and alarmed
Then you'll recognise me there standing open armed

Yes I see you there
Close enough to hold me
And I need you here
Wrap me in your arms
But I'm scared for you
I don't know the journey that you're going on

I believe your heart is pure
But I'm scared it's been fractured and torn apart
like a broken heart

Maybe you're not there
Maybe it's delusion
Just a stubborn man who'd never stop
Just a foolish father who could not face giving up

He rings the bell for his attendants.

Is it over now?
Perhaps I feel you've faded
For the years have passed
With nothing ever changed
I must make my plans
Farewell to this only only child of mine
Farewell to the child that never was

THE GREAT GAZOOMBEES [as Baron]
How was song?

KING GERARD
Hmm...

THE GREAT GAZOOMBEES [as Baron]
Feeling better?

KING GERARD
Marginal.

THE GREAT GAZOOMBEES [as Baron]
Marjorie?

KING GERARD
Marginal.

Doctor Chufflebanger enters.

DOCTOR CHUFFLEBANGER
You called, your majesty?

KING GERARD
These searches are futile. It's time to appoint a successor – from outside the family.

THE GREAT GAZOOMBEES
(To himself) Here we go!

KING GERARD
Dr Chufflebanger. We need applicants. Send word across the land.

DOCTOR CHUFFLEBANGER
Of course. I presume you would you like me to interview the candidates?

KING GERARD
Argh... ummm... well... no I think I'd like the baron to do that.

DOCTOR CHUFFLEBANGER
Sire, I must protest. This is Haile Selassie. For eighteen years I have kept silent and for eighteen years this man has been meddling in our affairs, filling the air with lies...

KING GERARD
...the Baron is my most trusted friend.

DOCTOR CHUFFLEBANGER
An honour your majesty that used to befall on me.

KING GERARD
Look at what he's done for this kingdom. He's designed a homogenous curvilinear sanitation system. He's totally remodelled our revolving moat with a fenestrated trunk shell.

THE GREAT GAZOOMBEES [as Baron]
And don't forget I'm working on the bilateral side-sparred cable-staid swing bridge.

KING GERARD
Pneumatic?

THE GREAT GAZOOMBEES [as Baron]
Of course.

DOCTOR CHUFFLEBANGER
Look at him, Sire. How is it that the years have taken their toll on all of us and yet he looks the same as he did eighteen years ago. (To The Great Gazoombees) In what dark arts do you dabble?

THE GREAT GAZOOMBEES [as Baron]
It's not my fault I have a beautiful Pilipotsian complexion. Maybe you should concentrate more on your job and less on my face.

DOCTOR CHUFFLEBANGER
Meaning?

THE GREAT GAZOOMBEES [as Baron]
The annual search parties. Year after year and you find nothing. Perhaps if I had been in charge…

DOCTOR CHUFFLEBANGER
I am committed to finding the Princess more than anyone. And I shall continue until the…

KING GERARD
You won't.

DOCTOR CHUFFLEBANGER
Your majesty.

KING GERARD
All future search parties are cancelled.

King Gerard exits.

DOCTOR CHUFFLEBANGER
I'm onto you!

THE GREAT GAZOOMBEES
(Winking) May the best man win… Chuffers!

The Great Gazoombees exits.

DOCTOR CHUFFLEBANGER
(In his face) Annual search party? I shall increase it to daily. I shall do it myself. I shall make it my mission.

SCENE 2
The Woods

Prince Corbyn comes to a clearing in the woods; backpack, rolled up quilt, lantern, egg whisk etc. He settles down for some respite, lights the lantern and hangs it on a tree. He gets out his diary and writes.

PRINCE CORBYN
Arrived at the border of Püss Püss - a peaceful and beautiful land; and far from my home in Nowen. *(Rubbing his feet)* The road was paved with thasps[50], but the rash on my bertie fishcakes[51] has now cleared, so having a shent[52] isn't so painful any more. Continue to be nervous about tomorrow's interview, had a little dobby dob[53] to calm myself down, but still no respite. Revise.

He puts down his diary and removes a piece of paper from his bag.

(Reading) Successor sought for ailing kingdom. Blah blah blah... Candidates should... blah blah... visionary leader. *(Puts the paper down)* Focus, Corbyn, focus. What are they

---

50 Hamster powered chariots.
51 An aggressive chaffinch.
52 A violent hiccup capable of dislodging a man's chestertons.
53 A hand based relaxation device.

going to ask? My geography's fine, history, arts, sports, science and nature... always a bit shaky on science and nature. Right. *(He opens a revision book)* What is the mating call of the bearded babasay[54]? Ah I know this... It's either *(accompanied by a gesture)* Skarama skarama skarama kooch, skarama skarama skarama kooch or *(accompanied by a different gesture)* dohhhhhhhhhhhhhhhhhhhhhhhhhhhhhhhhhhhhhhhh hhhh xhinee. If only there were humble woods-folk about to assist. *(Seeing the audience)* Oh, hello, there you are. Can you help? If you could all do it with me. Firstly; *(accompanied by a gesture)* skarama skarama skarama kooch, skarama skarama skarama kooch. Great. And now; *(accompanied by a different gesture)* dohhhhhhhhhhhhhhhhhhhhhhhhhhhhhhhhhhhhhhhh hhhh xhinee. Thanks, that definitely helps I've remembered it's *(accompanied by a gesture)* Skarama skarama skarama kooch, skarama skarama skarama kooch. Bearded babasay question two. The sound of this bird is extremely distressing to people from which region? Pilipots? Yes! Now, personal statement. How to sound confident without sounding cocky. Okay. My name is Prince Corbyn of the Dale, prince of Nowen. My redefined manifesto on Clause Four gained me the golden flenge[55]. I believe in the re-nationalisation of the

---

54 Celtic Goddess who sings theme tunes to branded spy films.

55 More Bakewell tart than Colin Jackson.

shenbalds[56], a free system of education and healthcare and rights for the common man. I have the passion and strength to deliver, to rule with a fair hand, to be the King of Püss Püss! Golly bensons[57], what if I do succeed? What good a throne without a Queen? 'Tis as barren as a feld without a wenge[58]. What good the humble art-snibbler[59] without its trusted malden-dew[60]? And what chance for the lesser spotted woowoosappa-woowoosappa[61] when spring cometh not like the cocking of her nadge[62].

SONG 7: GETTING TO KNOW YOU

Yes I'll need to find a lady to discourse with
to ponder all the trials and tales of life
She won't have to be a stunner
or a great long distance runner
but I'll be her husband and she'll be my wife

It won't matter if her name is Sue or Derek
Or her manner is a little hard to bear
Well her voice might be high pitched

---

56 Anything near or above Daventry.

57 In and of itself not that much, but who's counting.

58 An adverse camber sans slope.

59 A fancy cake with minimal toppings.

60 Moisture from adolescents.

61 A chequered mauve cockle.

62 A violent hiccup capable of dislodging a woman's or in this case a season's chestertons.

And she could even have a tick
But she'd be mine so then I'd hardly even care

Getting to know you, you and I together
We'll be braving any weather come what may
Getting to know you, holding hands and walking
We'll be talking and I'll love the things you say
Getting to know you, sailing on forever
There will never be another lonely day
For getting to know you means my life will be a dream
and that you'll never ever go away

There's so much to tell I hardly know your history
I listen as you tell me of your youth
Then I tell you all of mine
But really everything is fine
Because together's always better yes forsooth

We'll grow old and walk with sticks and fall asleep more
On that blanket where we'd snuggle underneath
Then you'll turn and call me Geoff
And then repeat it 'cause I'm deaf
Before you hand me that big jar with my false teeth

Getting to know you, you and I together
We'll be braving any weather come what may
Getting to know you, holding hands and walking
We'll be talking and I'll love the things you say
Getting to know you, sailing on forever
There will never be another lonely day

For getting to know you means my life will be a dream
and that you'll never ever go away
Yes getting to know you means my life will be a dream
and that you'll never ever go away

SCENE 3
Inside The Tower

Rapunzel is in her tower, she has ridiculously long flowing hair and glasses.

FAIRY 1 (V/O)
Our first glimpse of Rapunzel now, up in her tower.

FAIRY 2 (V/O)
We've waited a long time for this moment Fairy John – and she's certainly been a busy bee.

FAIRY 1 (V/O)
Beebee bu deebee. Reebee geebee. The Bee Gees of course nowhere to be seen. Rapunzel however very much staying alive.

FAIRY 2 (V/O)
Rapunzel the youngest qualified structural engineer in the land of Waa.

FAIRY 1 (V/O)
One might say... more than a woman.

FAIRY 2 (V/O)
Are you saying women can't be structural engineers?

FAIRY 1 (V/O)
I'm more trying to crowbar in another Bee Gees reference.

FAIRY 2 (V/O)
Please don't.

FAIRY 1 (V/O)
Do you love structural engineering, Fairy John?

FAIRY 2 (V/O)
Why do you ask?

FAIRY 1 (V/O)
I wondered, how deep is your love?

FAIRY 2 (V/O)
Okay! Let's get back to Rapunzel at this pivotal point in the game.

She goes to the window and lets her hair down but it doesn't quite reach the ground.

RAPUNZEL
Oh winston wilsterbays[63]! Just a few more days and it'll finally be long enough to climb down and explore this wondrous land of Waa.

She heads over to her desk and scribbles on engineering plans.

---

63 A childish alternative to the phrase "Oh Felicity, don't be such a Kendal!"

RAPUNZEL

Right back to work! Got to finish these blueprints. Now, the square root of minus three multiplied by Y times the substitution of gradient C is? Easy! Now to apply the kinetic force needed. Seven hundred newtons per square inch over the... oh come on it's not hard. I mean it's not as if it's a forward cantilevered gate swing opening single sided bridge; it's only a pneumatic, bilateral, side-spar cable-staid swing bridge. I mean really, piece of cake!

The Great Gazoombees enters with a package.

THE GREAT GAZOOMBEES

(Calling) My one and only! *(Seeing her)* My one and only!

RAPUNZEL

You're back!

THE GREAT GAZOOMBEES

(Touched) Indeed I am. And what does Daddy bring when he....

RAPUNZEL

Presents!

THE GREAT GAZOOMBEES

Present, actually, singular. We are living in a time of austerity, my one and only.

RAPUNZEL

Thank you so much Daddy. But I don't want presents. What I really want is just to... to.. argh!

THE GREAT GAZOOMBEES

...Woah woah woah, we've discussed this. Noise draws attention. Attention to the hunting parties...

RAPUNZEL

(knowing this off by heart) ...hunting parties that scour the land looking to snatch young girls like me. I know all that.

THE GREAT GAZOOMBEES

Everything I do is in your best interests. You know that don't you, my one and only?

RAPUNZEL

You tell me often enough. But I'm still stuck up here aren't I?

THE GREAT GAZOOMBEES

It's in your best interests.

RAPUNZEL

My best interests? In this tower? What if I think my best interests are down there. Yes I'm a fully qualified structural engineer with ISO 9001 certification specialising in hydrodynamic bridges with a quadrant fusion reaction core, but I really want is to see the world.

THE GREAT GAZOOMBEES

Come on my one and only, not now. Open your present. I know you'll like it.

RAPUNZEL

(Opening it, begrudgingly) It's not. *(She opens it)*

THE GREAT GAZOOMBEES

It is!

RAPUNZEL

The wetsuit!

THE GREAT GAZOOMBEES

The Neoprene Triple X one hundred with super stretch therma-core.

RAPUNZEL

And optional ear flaps?

THE GREAT GAZOOMBEES

And optional ear flaps.

RAPUNZEL

Thanks, Daddy.

THE GREAT GAZOOMBEES

Look, I know you're frustrated. But it's a cruel world out there. Only the most special little girls grow up under protection 'til they're older.

RAPUNZEL
How much older?

THE GREAT GAZOOMBEES
Remember that Daddy said he was assistant to the farmer who lives over yonder?

RAPUNZEL
Yes.

THE GREAT GAZOOMBEES
Well, very soon daddy's gonna be the head farmer and then you'll move in with daddy to the big farmhouse that looks like a palace and have all the parties and friends you like.

RAPUNZEL
(Unsure) I will?

THE GREAT GAZOOMBEES
And when you get there, you'll say that you're my long lost daughter from Pilipots.

RAPUNZEL
Pilipots. Why would I say that? You're from Pilipots. I'm from here.

THE GREAT GAZOOMBEES
Yeah but if people knew you were one of them 'special' girls locked in a tower they'd be ever so jealous and it would be very hard for you to make friends.

RAPUNZEL
Okay.

THE GREAT GAZOOMBEES
Have you finished the plans?

RAPUNZEL
Yes.

THE GREAT GAZOOMBEES
My friends at the pala… farm, will be very happy!

RAPUNZEL
I'll see you later, my one and only. *(Gives her a kiss)* Ooh, and I think we need to cut your hair soon. It's getting ever so long.

RAPUNZEL
(Over the top) No, daddy!

THE GREAT GAZOOMBEES
Alright, alright. Why such fuss?

RAPUNZEL
It's nothing, I just… like it long.

She flutters her eyelids at him.

THE GREAT GAZOOMBEES

(Shaking his head, won over) Wow, you could turn a lamb into a jackson[64] with them looks.

SONG 8: SET ME FREE

See the rooftops far away
The smoke from all the chimney's all I see
And I wonder who lives there
Would anybody want to talk to me
My mother told me that
Oh wait I never had a mom so it's a little weird to sing that line
But if I had a mum would she let me out to see the world and say go on and play
You will be fine

Set me Free, Let Me Go
There's more that I wanna know
Set me free, Let me go
Explore the world down below
Let me go oh oh oh etc

My daddy keeps me here inside
But what if all he told me is a lie?
Is the world so very cruel
Or am I just his one and only prize?

---

64 A cheesy chiropractor.

If I had a hundred tons of steel and a welding torch I could build a bridge
From here to the world outside

Set me Free, Let Me Go
There's more that I wanna know
Set me free, Let me go
Explore the world down below
Let me go oh oh oh etc

Go! Feel the roar of thunder
Go! Can't stay one day longer
Go! I can make it on my own on my own, here's a stone

Set me Free, Let Me Go
There's more that I wanna know
Set me free, Let me go
Explore the world down below
Let me go oh oh oh etc

SCENE 4
The Royal Palace

Prince Corbyn is being interviewed by The Great Gazoombees.

THE GREAT GAZOOMBEES [as Baron]
You certainly interview well. And you obviously have regal blood. Your explanation of the differences between the bearded and the shaved babasay is quite... *(he tails off in excitement)* But there is one final test. Seat please taking.

PRINCE CORBYN
Of course.

THE GREAT GAZOOMBEES [as Baron]
Simple word association. I say word, you say word, first thing that comes into your head. There is no right or wrong.

PRINCE CORBYN
Right.

THE GREAT GAZOOMBEES [as Baron]
What?

PRINCE CORBYN
Right.

THE GREAT GAZOOMBEES [as Baron]
No. There is no right or wrong.

PRINCE CORBYN
Understood.

THE GREAT GAZOOMBEES [as Baron]
Right!

They both laugh.

THE GREAT GAZOOMBEES [as Baron]
Fnaaazg[65].

PRINCE CORBYN
Shlurp[66].

THE GREAT GAZOOMBEES [as Baron]
Interesting. *(He writes something down)* Bodokai[67].

PRINCE CORBYN
Yaelinmommo[68].

THE GREAT GAZOOMBEES [as Baron]
Yes! *(He writes something down)* ShaShaShaShaShaaaaaa Loco[69].

---

65 Osteopath.

66 Topiary.

67 Toe hair.

68 British Rail.

69 Braised haddock.

PRINCE CORBYN
Rusha-mantî. Fø[70].

THE GREAT GAZOOMBEES [as Baron]
Fascinating. *(He writes something down)* Glweton[71].

PRINCE CORBYN
Plong[72].

THE GREAT GAZOOMBEES [as Baron]
Rondon[73].

PRINCE CORBYN
Kemp[74].

THE GREAT GAZOOMBEES [as Baron]
Quelsaaaa[75].

PRINCE CORBYN
Flip[76].

---

70 Colostomy rucksacks.

71 Brian Blessed.

72 E=MC Hammer

73 Spatula.

74 Spartacus.

75 Thermal Y-fronts.

76 Shipping forecasts.

They continue getting faster and faster until they merge, holding a sound, until The Great Gazoombees breaks[77].

THE GREAT GAZOOMBEES [as Baron]
You were brilliant.

PRINCE CORBYN
Really?

THE GREAT GAZOOMBEES [as Baron]
Pfft. Unique. Natural. So. We have your address?

PRINCE CORBYN
I didn't bring a dress.

THE GREAT GAZOOMBEES [as Baron]
No problem. We can provide. I'll be in touch.

PRINCE CORBYN
Thank you. What do you think my chances are of being…

THE GREAT GAZOOMBEES [as Baron]
(Violently silencing him) …Arsène Venger. *(Ushering him to the door)* There's a great many candidates to see. But, you did good.

---

[77] The entire section above is a classic early Jungian personality test - the more astute will notice 'plong' utilised here as a trick word, the appropriate response clearly being 'Benny Biddles Jenson'.

PRINCE CORBYN
Well.

THE GREAT GAZOOMBEES [as Baron]
Well what?

PRINCE CORBYN
You did 'well'.

THE GREAT GAZOOMBEES [as Baron]
Thank you. Now leave.

The Great Gazoombees closes the door on him and rips up his CV.

The door opens and King Gerard walks in.

KING GERARD
Hello old chap. Interviews eh? Still no joy?

THE GREAT GAZOOMBEES [as Baron]
They are all terrible. Alack the day.

KING GERARD
Yes... yes... Aled Jones.

THE GREAT GAZOOMBEES [as Baron]
And at sunrise the deadline for applications is up. I only wish there was something I could do.

KING GERARD
Well, there is something you could do actually. It's rather been staring me in the face this whole time.

THE GREAT GAZOOMBEES [as Baron]
Sire?

KING GERARD
This applicant, succession malarky... you say it's not really, you know... and, well, here's the thing – if nobody suitable has been found by tomorrow morning, I would really like you to be my successor.

THE GREAT GAZOOMBEES [as Baron]
Your majesty. I would not have the first idea of how to be King.

KING GERARD
Oh colly johnsons[78]. You practically run the place anyway.

THE GREAT GAZOOMBEES [as Baron]
No, no, no it's not just me, it is mainly me, but also you, not really you so much to be fair, but I mustn't take all the credit, although most people would, it would be an honour.

---

78 An old fashioned way of expressing the difference between identical vicars.

KING GERARD
(Producing a scroll) Here's the royal decree, I'll sign it in the morning and away we go – assuming of course no last minute candidates emerge. I must say that's quite a shoop off my bipps[79].

THE GREAT GAZOOMBEES [as Baron]
Gaaaree Linekoo.

KING GERARD
(General muttering) Hmm, yes.

THE GREAT GAZOOMBEES [as Baron]
June Invaaadal.

KING GERARD
(General muttering) Ah, yes yes.

THE GREAT GAZOOMBEES [as Baron]
And Clare Booouuulding.

KING GERARD
(General muttering) Quite.

---

79 An expression of relief similar to having a fabulous dobby dob.

THE GREAT GAZOOMBEES [as Baron]
Back in my land, when one is bestowed an honour of this magnitude, we have a very special way to show our gratitude.

He approaches King Gerard, who backs off nervously at The Great Gazoombees' sudden sexual tension.

KING GERARD
No no, that's quite alright. I'm well aware of your shows of gratitude...

THE GREAT GAZOOMBEES [as Baron]
Come to me! *(Advancing)* Rum pa-pa-pum... Rum pa-pa-pum...

KING GERARD
(Backing out the door) ...Yes yes, lovely, very good, very good.

The Great Gazoombees slaps his bum on the way out and shuts the door.

KING GERARD
Ooh!

The Great Gazoombees takes centre stage and does an elaborate bow to his imaginary audience.

SCENE 5
Outside the Tower

Rapunzel jumps down from the tower, complete with wet suit and mask. She removes the diving apparel and with a little cockle knife cuts off the trail of hair that hangs down from the top. She puts the remainder of her hair up inside a cap, then tugs on the long trailing hair to check it's still secure.

RAPUNZEL
Sorry Daddy, a girl's gotta do what a girl's gotta do. Earth at last.

She falls to her knees, excited, nervous…

RAPUNZEL
The ground it feels so… so warm… thermal dynamics give the ground such warmth, yet the irrigational qualities of the earth deliver remarkable hydration – a perfect environment in which to eco-friendly multifunctional monolith, or some or other such like structure.

A bar of music, she takes a breath to sing…

PRINCE CORBYN (*Off*)
I nailed the question on the history of Waa…

RAPUNZEL
Yes! A person!

She withdraws. Prince Corbyn enters.

PRINCE CORBYN
...and they loved my bearded babasay impression. It seemed to go well... I mean I don't want to get too... Time will tell.

Prince Corbyn puts his bags down and starts carving a small twig. He briefly turns away from the audience and when he turns back the twig is now a fully formed ukulele. He finds another twig and starts carving. He briefly turns away and when he turns back the twig is now a fully formed mouth organ. He thinks. He finds another twig and starts carving once more. He briefly turns away and when he turns back the twig is now an odd looking pole. He fastens the pole to the mouth organ and the ukulele to the pole. He's about to play, but thinks better of it. He goes to his bags and gets out a miniature drum kit and starts to tune up. Rapunzel enters and seeing the ukulele-mouth-organ combo picks it up and considers it.

PRINCE CORBYN
One, two, one, two, three, four.

Simultaneously they start playing a musical number in perfect harmony. Prince Corbyn notices Rapunzel and smiles. She reciprocates. They continue as they chat, like awkward teenagers.

PRINCE CORBYN
Chutney Bishops you're good!

RAPUNZEL
Chutney Bishops *you're* good!

PRINCE CORBYN
Not as good as you.

RAPUNZEL
You flatter me.

PRINCE CORBYN
Perhaps you're worth flattering.

RAPUNZEL
You saying I'm not good?

PRINCE CORBYN
(To himself) Bad choice of words Corbyn!

RAPUNZEL
Just kidding!

PRINCE CORBYN
Oh phew!

The music ends.

PRINCE CORBYN

Oh sorry how rude of me *(He hands her a business card)* Prince Corbyn of Nowen. The shell[80] is silent.

RAPUNZEL

I noticed.

PRINCE CORBYN

Many don't.

RAPUNZEL

How could you not?

PRINCE CORBYN

You'd be surprised.

RAPUNZEL

When?

PRINCE CORBYN

When I do this. *(he does a silly gesture)*

Music starts again…

PRINCE CORBYN

Chutney Bishops you're good.

---

80 An elusive and silent diphthong that is wont to surprise congregations at Evensong. Rhymes with 'bench'.

RAPUNZEL

Chutney Bishops *you're* good.

PRINCE CORBYN

Not as good as you.

RAPUNZEL

You flatter me.

PRINCE CORBYN

Perhaps you're worth flattering.

RAPUNZEL

You saying I'm not good?

PRINCE CORBYN

(To himself) Bad choice of words Corbyn!

RAPUNZEL

Just kidding!

PRINCE CORBYN

Oh phew!

The music ends.

PRINCE CORBYN

Oh sorry how rude of me *(He hands her a business card)* Prince Corbyn of Nowen. The shell is silent.

RAPUNZEL
Have we been here before?

PRINCE CORBYN
I'm not sure. Have we?

RAPUNZEL
I don't know. Chutney Bishops I'm nervous.

PRINCE CORBYN
Chutney Bishops, I'm nervous too.

Music starts again. They get faster and faster though the next section. More and more furious and excited…

PRINCE CORBYN
Chutney Bishops you're good.

RAPUNZEL
Chutney Bishops *you're* good.

PRINCE CORBYN
Not as good as you.

RAPUNZEL
You flatter me.

PRINCE CORBYN
Perhaps you're worth flattering.

RAPUNZEL
You saying I'm not good?

PRINCE CORBYN
(To himself) Bad choice of words Corbyn!

RAPUNZEL
Just kidding!

PRINCE CORBYN
Oh phew!

As the music ends with a final climax.

PRINCE CORBYN
So, what's your name?

RAPUNZEL
My one and only.

PRINCE CORBYN
Yeah, okay your one and only name!

RAPUNZEL
No no, that's my name.

PRINCE CORBYN
What is?

RAPUNZEL
My one and only.

PRINCE CORBYN
Your one and only name?

RAPUNZEL
Yes.

PRINCE CORBYN
Is?

RAPUNZEL
My one and only.

PRINCE CORBYN
I think we've got off on the wrong foot.

They shift their balance from their left to right feet.

PRINCE CORBYN
That's better. What's your name?

RAPUNZEL
My one and only.

PRINCE CORBYN

Holy fadanbas[81]. I'll try another question. *(Pointing at the hanging hair)* What's with the hair?

RAPUNZEL

Oh that's mine.

PRINCE CORBYN

(Confused) Right.

RAPUNZEL

(Pointing) I've been living up there, but I've decided to come down here.

PRINCE CORBYN

(Still confused) Okay.

RAPUNZEL

For the very first time.

PRINCE CORBYN

Pardon?

RAPUNZEL

By climbing down my hair.

PRINCE CORBYN

What?

---

81 The early onset of excessive soup syndrome.

RAPUNZEL

I've been living up there but I've decided to...

PRINCE CORBYN

No I heard you, I'm just a little... You've been living up there?

RAPUNZEL

Oh yes!

PRINCE CORBYN

Ah! Crondont[82]! For a holiday.

RAPUNZEL

No, no. Forever.

PRINCE CORBYN

Forever? In that tiny tower?

RAPUNZEL

In a room at the top.

PRINCE CORBYN

And you've never been down?

RAPUNZEL

I have now.

---

82 Preposterous levels of laminated checklists.

PRINCE CORBYN

So you've lived all your life in a room at the top of a tower in the middle of nowhere and you've never been out and you've climbed down your hair and you don't even know your name. You must be what, eighteen? Oh my golly bensons, you're Rapunzel!

RAPUNZEL

Who?

PRINCE CORBYN

Come to think of it you do look like her!

RAPUNZEL

Like who?

PRINCE CORBYN

The paintings of the old Queen.

RAPUNZEL

What queen?

PRINCE CORBYN

So where's the witch?

RAPUNZEL

Which witch?

DOCTOR CHUFFLEBANGER (*Off*)
Ordinance Rembez[83] section six.

PRINCE CORBYN
Quick. Hide.

They disappear and Doctor Chufflebanger enters with a massive map.

DOCTOR CHUFFLEBANGER
An uncharted edifice. *(She looks up at the tower and down again at the map)* A tower!

PRINCE CORBYN (*Off*)
Is that her?

RAPUNZEL (*Off*)
Who?

DOCTOR CHUFFLEBANGER
After all these years!

PRINCE CORBYN (*Off*)
The witch?

---

83 Rembez: Deep pastel hue created by whisking an egg whisk with giraffe cream and vimto. Ordinance Rembez: a sponge sized edible map of that shade.

RAPUNZEL (*Off*)
Which witch?

DOCTOR CHUFFLEBANGER
Could it be?

Prince Corbyn steps out.

PRINCE CORBYN
Get back witch. I am afeared not of your potions, lotions and spells.

DOCTOR CHUFFLEBANGER
Me witch. You witch. Who are you calling a witch, witch?

PRINCE CORBYN
What?

DOCTOR CHUFFLEBANGER
Which?

PRINCE CORBYN
Who goes there?

DOCTOR CHUFFLEBANGER
Nay, who goes *there*?

PRINCE CORBYN
I am the guardian of what lies in that tower.

DOCTOR CHUFFLEBANGER

Then I am your sworn enemy for what lies in that tower belongs not to you!

PRINCE CORBYN

Quite. Couldn't agree more. Prince Corbyn of Nowen. The shell is silent.

DOCTOR CHUFFLEBANGER

Doctor Chufflebanger, Royal Medic to the court of Püss Püss.

PRINCE CORBYN

Ah! Then I have information for you regarding the whereabouts of Princess Rapunzel.

DOCTOR CHUFFLEBANGER

You do? Where?

PRINCE CORBYN

Where do I have the information, or where are the whereabouts of Princess Rapunzel?

DOCTOR CHUFFLEBANGER

(Confused) Either. Both.

PRINCE CORBYN

Right, the information's here *(points to his head)* and the princess is there.

DOCTOR CHUFFLEBANGER
Oh good.

Rapunzel slowly emerges from the shadows.

DOCTOR CHUFFLEBANGER
Rapunzel! Rapunzel? *(Looking her up and down)* Let down your hair. *(She removes her cap and lets down her hair)* It is you. You look just like her.

RAPUNZEL
Like who?

DOCTOR CHUFFLEBANGER
We'll talk about this later. Where's the witch?

RAPUNZEL
What is it with this witch obsession! It's just me and my Daddy…

THE GREAT GAZOOMBEES (Off)
(Singing) See 'The Great Gazoombees' and better your life…

RAPUNZEL
That's him now.

DOCTOR CHUFFLEBANGER
Your daddy? Indeed. I'll handle this. *(To Prince Corbyn)* Take her. Hide in yonder woods, I will meet you there anon.

Prince Corbyn hurries off with Rapunzel. The Great Gazoombees enters, seeing the long trail of hair hanging from the tower.

THE GREAT GAZOOMBEES
(Calling out) My one and only! My one and only!...

He falls to the floor.

DOCTOR CHUFFLEBANGER
(Incredulous) It was you!?

THE GREAT GAZOOMBEES
(Ignoring Doctor Chufflebanger) Where did you go, little girl. I told you to stay. We were so close. A few more days and we would have had everything.

DOCTOR CHUFFLEBANGER
It's over.

THE GREAT GAZOOMBEES
(Looking up at Doctor Chufflebanger for the first time) Where is she?

DOCTOR CHUFFLEBANGER
She's safe, now. She will return to the palace, as the rightful heir. And you, you will face your rightful judgement.

THE GREAT GAZOOMBEES

Oh will I? And you're gonna take me in are you, all on your Timmy Todds[84]? What you gonna do, doctor, throw a book at me? Beat me up with your qualifications? Study me to death? You forget, Chuffers, you're from the library – I'm from the street.

The Great Gazoombees puts his hand in his pocket and draws out a sharp implement with which he slashes Doctor Chufflebanger on her face. He steps back, alarmed.

DOCTOR CHUFFLEBANGER

You certainly behave like a street ruffian. Have you no sense of justice, no moral fibre, not an ounce of…

THE GREAT GAZOOMBEES

Oh I don't need any of that doctor. You see, the tables have turned!

DOCTOR CHUFFLEBANGER

Revolving tables. I've never heard of such a thing.

THE GREAT GAZOOMBEES

No, you lemsip. *(Referring to his cheek)* A mere scratch…

---

[84] Not often but quite possibly.

DOCTOR CHUFFLEBANGER

Amir Kahn[85]?

THE GREAT GAZOOMBEES

...a mere scratch but infused with Dram-raks. The very same herb with which I poisoned the Queen.

DOCTOR CHUFFLEBANGER

Why you..!

THE GREAT GAZOOMBEES

Even the slightest amount will have you asleep for days; and by the time you wake – I'll be King!

DOCTOR CHUFFLEBANGER

(Putting her hand to her face) What? No...

THE GREAT GAZOOMBEES

And as there's no Rapunzel herb to save you *(he dangles his stash in front of her)*, seems like it's your bedtime Chuffers. Three... two... one...

Doctor Chufflebanger falls to the floor.

---

85 Not to be confused with Amir Khan the English professional boxer and former two time world champion, having won the WBA, WBA and IBF Light Welterweight titles.

THE GREAT GAZOOMBEES
Nighty night!

The Great Gazoombees rushes off. The Doctor's hand goes up and pulls down the hair which falls from the tower. She lies on the floor, chewing the hair…

SCENE 6
The Woods

Rapunzel and Prince Corbyn are waiting for Doctor Chufflebanger elsewhere in the woods. Night is falling.

PRINCE CORBYN
… then there *you* were in the middle of the forest.

RAPUNZEL
It's all so confusing…

PRINCE CORBYN
(Impatient) Come on, Doctor!

RAPUNZEL
…There's my new family, my old family, my mother I never knew… What was she like? Was she a good ruler? A ruler? A princess. A palace. A queen. That's means I'll be.. I'll be… How can I be…

PRINCE CORBYN
(Violently silencing him) …Arsène Venger! *(Rapunzel stops and looks at him. He smiles. Sweetly)* You know what I always do to calm down when I'm anxious and flustered?

RAPUNZEL
No, what do you always do to calm down when you're anxious and flustered?

PRINCE CORBYN
I have a little dobby dob.

RAPUNZEL
A dobby dob?

PRINCE CORBYN
Yes. Have you ever…?

RAPUNZEL
I've solo dobbed. But I've never… you know…with someone else. Have you?

PRINCE CORBYN
Yeah not for a while but yeah sure.

(Pause)

RAPUNZEL
Uh… So…?

PRINCE CORBYN
Yeah…

RAPUNZEL
Should we…?

PRINCE CORBYN / RAPUNZEL
Dobby Dob?

(Pause)

RAPUNZEL

Have you got a French Bishop[86]?

PRINCE CORBYN

Absolutely. I always safe Dob.

He gets out two medical gloves and they each put one on their left hand. They stand and perform the Waltz of the Dobby Dobs[87], a beautiful romantic choreographed hand-based dance. She makes a wrong move.

RAPUNZEL

Oh Crembez[88]! I dobbed prematurely.

PRINCE CORBYN

Don't worry it happens to us all.

RAPUNZEL

But I messed it up.

---

86 Prophylactic gloves.

87 As 'Dobby dob' but with Bruce Forsyth ever present.

88 Those familiar with Nowenthian vocabulary will recall, from Jack and The Beanstalk, the translation as 'A flexible exclamation keen on yoga.' In Püss Püss however, Crembez is more akin to the surprise one would experience if one found a dentist in one's soup.

PRINCE CORBYN

Not at all. I think that you are...

RAPUNZEL

(Violently silencing him) ...Arsène Venger.

PRINCE CORBYN

But I really, really...

RAPUNZEL

...No you don't... You think you do now because it's fresh and exciting and I play a mean ukulele but when you get to know me you'll start to feel differently, you'll realise I'm just awkward. I really... you. But you wouldn't really... me? I mean, I can't even Dobby Dob properly. Loving me would be.. it would be... be just...

SONG 9: LIGHTNING STORM

PRINCE CORBYN

Loving you is easy
Loving you's inviting
Loving you's exciting
It's a lighting storm

Feel that I have woken
Every word you've spoken
Swirls around my head
Like electricity

A lightning storm
Stronger than you'll ever know
Takes away your heart's control
Maybe I can be your thunderbolt
Lighting never strikes the same place
Grab this chance to start the race together

RAPUNZEL
Seeing you is thrilling
Holding you so chilling
Feeling you within me
Like a whirlwind

Thinking words then talking
Stepping out and walking
Every stage I tremble
Like the leaves beneath the wind

BOTH
A lightning storm
Stronger than you'll ever know
Takes away your heart's control
Maybe I can be your thunderbolt
Lighting never strikes the same place
Grab this chance to start the race together

RAPUNZEL

Dibble on your Dobson[89]

PRINCE CORBYN

Nibble on your Nobsons[90]

RAPUNZEL

Gibble on my mampass[91]

PRINCE CORBYN

Like a fedge within a crall[92]

RAPUNZEL

She's giving me a Sebe[93]

PRINCE CORBYN

I feel it in my Debe[94]

RAPUNZEL

Touch my hanging Jacksons

---

89 To stretch profusely.

90 If you can reach them then crack on.

91 Under health and safety legislation, always advisable after nibbling on your nobsons.

92 An idiom similar to 'Where's my duster?'

93 Sudden rush of adolescent fluids

94 Elbow based erroneous zone (fees may apply)

PRINCE CORBYN

And I'll place them in my podge[95]

BOTH

A lightning storm
Stronger than you'll ever know
Takes away your heart's control
Maybe I can be your thunderbolt
Lighting never strikes the same place
Grab this chance to start the race together
You and me together – we'll be a lighting storm

They kiss.

RAPUNZEL

Wow, that beats dobby dobbing hands down!

PRINCE CORBYN

Something's happened to the Doctor. We're not safe. Come, if we hurry now we can get to the palace by day break.

RAPUNZEL

(Exiting) Have you ever double dibbie dobbied[96]?

---

95 Heart.

96 See BBC1's hit show Strictly Dobbing.

SCENE 7
The Royal Palace

A puff of smoke and two fairy puppets appear.

FAIRY 1
Well, double dibby dobby. A dibby dabble dabby.

FAIRY 2
Absolutely.

FAIRY 1
We're entering the final stages of the championship now. And surely it must all be over soon.

FAIRY 2
I would certainly hope so.

FAIRY 1
The King back at court – in fact you could say in court on court, as he plays another round of riggeddy ding dong. Dingy dingy dungee... Dungee Makwenbe[97] of course the twice runner up here.

KING GERARD
(Shouting off) Nice game, Dungee. Oh by the way where did you get those shorts? Fabulous. Fabulous. Aren't they a

---

97 Dungee Redmaine Cumberbatch, current world champion of riggeddy ding dong.

little tight around the uh... No, no... snug. Snug! Yes. Fancy meeting me by the big window tomorrow for a cup of tea and a Ferrero Rocher? Dungee? Oh, gone! Strange chap!

Prince Corbyn enters.

PRINCE CORBYN
Excuse me, Sire? Sorry to interrupt.

KING GERARD
Oh is it time? Already!?

PRINCE CORBYN
No, Sire it's not...

KING GERARD
...yes nothing like of early morning riggeddy ding dong to get the rondos running through your quenth. Pick up a ding.

PRINCE CORBYN
No, no, I have important business.

KING GERARD
Yes well no business on the riggeddy ding dong court. Your serve or mine?

Prince Corbyn picks up a racket.

PRINCE CORBYN
Please.

KING GERARD

Jolly pencils[98].

King Gerard serves and they start to rally…

PRINCE CORBYN

I must speak with you, your majesty.

KING GERARD

Must you?

PRINCE CORBYN

Yes. Good shot, Sire.

KING GERARD

Thank you I've been working on that one.

King Gerard serves again and they start to rally…

PRINCE CORBYN

It's a family matter, really.

KING GERARD

Very good. Are we related?

PRINCE CORBYN

Not exactly. But I…

---

98 Similar yet vastly different to a Chinese takeaway.

KING GERARD

Come to think of it, you do look a little like cousin Billy's boy. Strange fellow, walks with a limp. Lost his arm in a pompom accident. Terrific shot, old boy.

King Gerard serves again and they start to rally…

PRINCE CORBYN

No, Sire…

KING GERARD

Be about the same age as my daughter, were she still alive.

PRINCE CORBYN

That's just it. I've found her!

KING GERARD

Hmm, found who?

PRINCE CORBYN

Your daughter. Rapunzel.

King Gerard's ball spins out and crashes through a window shattering the glass.

KING GERARD

Rapunzel?

Rapunzel steps forward.

RAPUNZEL
Father?

KING GERARD
Well, no no, look here. I'm not sure... *(To Prince Corbyn)* Who are you?

The Great Gazoombees enters.

THE GREAT GAZOOMBEES [as Baron]
Impostors, Sire. Trying to gain the throne.

RAPUNZEL
(To The Great Gazoombees) Daddy?

PRINCE CORBYN
Daddy?

KING GERARD
Daddy? What's going on?

RAPUNZEL
Why are you talking in that strange voice?

THE GREAT GAZOOMBEES [as Baron]
I do not know this girl.

RAPUNZEL
What?

THE GREAT GAZOOMBEES [as Baron]
But I have seen this man before. He interviewed for the yob of King.

KING GERARD
The what?

THE GREAT GAZOOMBEES [as Baron]
The yob of King.

KING GERARD
Yob? Oh Job! Yes, yes.

THE GREAT GAZOOMBEES [as Baron]
One of the worst candidates we had…

PRINCE CORBYN
(Protesting) Now look here!

RAPUNZEL
Daddy, what are you..?

KING GERARD
Take them to the dungeons!

THE GREAT GAZOOMBEES [as Baron]
…and now you stoop so low as to try and gain the throne by lies and deception.

Doctor Chufflebanger enters, strands of hair trailing from her mouth.

DOCTOR CHUFFLEBANGER
It is you who is the master of lies and *(spitting out some hair)* deception.

THE GREAT GAZOOMBEES
How did you?

KING GERARD
Chuffers?

THE GREAT GAZOOMBEES
I thought I...?

DOCTOR CHUFFLEBANGER
Poisoned me. With the very same Dram-raks herb that poisoned the Queen?

They gasp.

THE GREAT GAZOOMBEES
But I'm the only one with the antidote.

DOCTOR CHUFFLEBANGER
That may appear to be the case. But any studied doctor would know that the traces of the herbs administered before

birth would be infused in the child's D.N.Ooskus[99]. All I had to do *(spitting the last bits out)* was munch on Rapunzel's hair.

ALL
You mean?

DOCTOR CHUFFLEBANGER
Yes. Munch on Rapunzel's hair.

KING GERARD
So...?

DOCTOR CHUFFLEBANGER
There was no witch. It was the Baron all along, he made the Queen ill then cured her with the Rapunzel herb so you would feel indebted to him.

KING GERARD
Why you...!

THE GREAT GAZOOMBEES
Too late. As of today I am the King. *(Holding the scroll in his hand)* All I need is your final signature here!

KING GERARD
My signature ear? No, not my signature ear. Take the other one.

---

99 The key to mankind's closeted skeletons.

THE GREAT GAZOOMBEES

No you lemsip. Sign here!

KING GERARD

You'll never get me to sign.

THE GREAT GAZOOMBEES

(Grabbing King Gerard and holding a knife to his throat) Oh, won't I? Sign!

PRINCE CORBYN

Just a quick question. Before you do that… does the button on your left cuff contain an indentation or other forms of markings in the right hand corner? No, I thought not. You see buttons and other haberdashery items are the chief export of Pilipots. When sent outside the region they're stamped with indentations on the rim, but when traded locally are left unstamped and without markings. Yours contain no such markings, ergo you bought your clothing in Pilipots – and judging by the age of the weave you most likely grew up there, perhaps the son of a haberdasher. Therefore being a Pilipotsian you panic on hearing the mating call of the bearded babasay.

THE GREAT GAZOOMBEES

Go on then, knock yourself out!

PRINCE CORBYN

Skarama skarama skarama kooch, skarama skarama skarama kooch.

THE GREAT GAZOOMBEES

Nice try, but I've trained myself to endure the solitary mating calls of the bearded babasay.

PRINCE CORBYN

Solitary maybe. But how about communal?

PRINCE CORBYN

(Looking to the other characters and audience to help in the call) Skarama skarama skarama kooch, skarama skarama skarama kooch

ALL APART FROM THE GREAT GAZOOMBEES

Skarama skarama skarama kooch, skarama skarama skarama kooch

The Great Gazoombees screams in pain, drops the knife and raises his hands to his ears.

KING GERARD

(Indicating Rapunzel) So this really is…?

DOCTOR CHUFFLEBANGER

Yes.

KING GERARD

Rapunzel? Rapunzel? Let down your hair, child. *(She takes off her cap and does so)* You look just like your mother. *(Of The Great Gazoombees)* Take him to the dungeons.

RAPUNZEL
No, wait. He's not so bad. It's hard being a single parent in an isolated tower in the middle of nowhere, but he did the best he could. Breast fed me from a young age, brought me everything I wanted – books, games, scuba diving equipment. He gave love in the only way he knew.

THE GREAT GAZOOMBEES
Forgive me for I knew not what I done. With each step I plunged further into the mire. As she grew she reminded me of myself when I was little. Innocent, curious, with a love for scuba diving. I was so...

The sound fades out as two fairy puppets appear. The actors continue to mime the scene under the narration of the fairies – either in a overly dramatic way or in a way that bears no resemblance to what the fairies are saying.

FAIRY 2 (V/O)
Sensational outcome there.

FAIRY 1 (V/O)
The Baron certainly played the long game – and it almost paid off. Man of the match, Fairy John?

FAIRY 2 (V/O)
It's gotta be the doctor. Hats off to her. Chastised, admonished, reputation in tatters, they questioned her integrity but she's remained true throughout. And it's so good to see a clean competitor in fairytales nowadays.

FAIRY 1 (V/O)

And it seems that good triumphs over evil and the baron is forgiven. That's a lot to forgive, surely?

FAIRY 2 (V/O)

Well we've seen it before and we'll certainly see it again.

FAIRY 1 (V/O)

Rapunzel of course, very much the underdog at the start of the proceedings, lived happily with her husband Prince Corbyn. They had many healthy children together, their children had children, their children also had children, their children's children had children and one of those children had a beard.

FAIRY 2 (V/O)

The King could end his days at peace, the memory of his lost bride living on in his beautiful daughter, Rapunzel.

FAIRY 1 (V/O)

As for the baron – he was allowed visiting rights, every third Sunday; but always under the ever watchful eye of the noble Doctor Chufflebanger.

FAIRY 2 (V/O)

And of course we'll be back in the land of Waa at the same time next year.

FAIRY 1 (V/O)

Until then, good people of Finsbury Park, we'll leave you with the traditional Champions toast.

SONG 10: MEDLEY

ALL

Partners, what it's all about
Partners, what a team
Partners we're the perfect match
A partnershipping dream

RAPUNZEL & PRINCE CORBYN

Getting to know you, you and I together
We'll be braving any weather come what may
Getting to know you, holding hands and walking
We'll be talking and I'll love the things you say
Getting to know you, sailing on forever
There will never be another lonely day
For getting to know you means my life will be a dream
and that you'll never ever go away

ALL

Shentel!

RAPUNZEL [Spoken]

Thank you, good people of Püss Püss, for coming here to give Shentel on this jubilant day. In return we would like to offer Shentel to you. So big birthday love to [names on her card] and a royal shout-out to [names on her card].

ALL
Jubilation at the coming of the heir apparent yes it's
Jubilation the return of the royal child
Jubilation throwing parties all across the land so full of
Jubilation Jubilation Jubilation

ALL
(Encouraging the audience to join the Chorus)
Jubilation at the coming of the heir apparent yes it's
Jubilation the return of the royal child
Jubilation throwing parties all across the land so full of
Jubilation Jubilation Jubilation
Jubilation at the coming of the heir apparent yes it's
Jubilation the return of the royal child
Jubilation throwing parties all across the land so full of
Jubilation Jubilation Jubilation

A confetti canon fires…

BOWS

The actors take their bow.

The actors signal to the Fairy puppets who take their bow.

The actors signal to cardboard cut-outs of the following actors, along with name tags to accompany them, who take their bow: Arsène Venger, Haile Selassie, Aled Jones and Gary Lineker, John Inverdale and Clare Balding.

Score

Jubilation

Song 1: (Act1, Sc1)

Music and Lyrics by Jez Bond

Arrangement by Dimitri Scarlato

©

F C F
Ju - bi - la - tion at the co - ming of heir ap - pa - rent yes it's Ju - bi - la - tion at the co - ming of a
Pno.
C F C
ro - yal child - Ju - bi - la - tion throw - ing par - ties all a - cross the land so full of
Pno.
F G C Dmin7 Emin7 F G C Dmin7 Emin7
Ju - bi - la - tion Ju - bi - la - tion Ju - bi - la - tion Ju - bi - la - tion Ju - bi - la - tion Ju - bi - la - tion
Pno.
Freely
Doctor Chufflebanger
G7#5b9 C7#9 G7#5b9 C7#9
Our li - ne - age con - ti - nues The ol - dest fa - mi - ly in Waa
All
Vox.
Waa Waa Waa Waa Waa
Pno.

King Gerard
C7
F13
F13
C7♯9
Noble and fair and just their ru - ling And now peo-ple travel ve-ry far
Vox.
far far far far far
Pno.
C7
G7♯5b9
F13
C7
To give their
Pno.
F
C
F
Ju - bi - la - tion at the co-ming of heir ap - pa - rent yes it's Ju - bi - la - tion at the co-ming of a
Vox.
Ju - bi - la - tion at the co-ming of heir ap - pa - rent yes it's Ju - bi - la - tion at the co-ming of a
Pno.

C F C
40
ro - yal child - Ju - bi - la - tion throw - ing par - ties all a - cross the land so full of
Vox.
Pno.
F G C Dmin7 Emin7 F C
43
Ju - bi - la - tion Ju - bi - la - tion Ju - bi - la - tion Ju - bi - la - tion at the co - ming of heir ap - pa - rent yes it's
F C F
47
Ju - bi - la - tion at the co - ming of a ro - yal child - Ju - bi - la - tion throw - ing par - ties all a -

C F G C Dmin7 Emin7 F G
50
cross the land___ so full of Ju - bi-la-tion Ju - bi-la-tion Ju - bi - la - tion Ju - bi-la-tion Ju - bi-la-tion
Vox.
cross the land___ so full of Ju - bi-la-tion Ju - bi-la-tion Ju - bi - la - tion Ju - bi-la-tion Ju - bi-la-tion
50
Pno.
C Dmin7 Emin7 F G C Dmin7 Emin7
54
Ju - bi - la - tion Ju - bi-la-tion Ju - bi-la-tion Ju - bi - la - tion
Vox.
Ju - bi - la - tion Ju - bi-la-tion Ju - bi-la-tion Ju - bi - la - tion
54
Pno.
F G C Dmin7 Emin7
57
Ju - bi - la - tion Ju - bi - la - tion Ju - bi - la - tion
Vox.
Ju - bi - la - tion Ju - bi - la - tion Ju - bi - la - tion
57
Pno.

Score

The Great Gazoombees

Sond 2: (Act1,Sc 2)

Music and Lyrics by Jez bond
Arrangement by Dimitri Scarlato

THE GREAT GAZOOMBEES
G7
If your knees a-ching If your fe-ver's bak-ing If your skin is fla-king
Pno.
G7
There's a lit-le cure here for you Sold that to a ro-yal She was aw-ful-ly lo-yal
Pno.
Cured her na-sty boil Ne-ver wa-tered down one per-
Pno.
spoken
Cmin
DOB. & GREAT GAZ.
G7
cent I pre-fer to think of it as wa-tered up See 'The Great Ga-zoo-bees' And bet-ter your
Pno.

Cmin
Cmin
life Take a-way pain Take a-way strife See "The Great Ga-zoo-bees' And
Pno.
G7
Cmin
THE GREAT GAZOOMBEES
bet-ter your life He's the on-ly man to do it for you If you'reneed-ing
Pno.
G7
tooth floss Suf-fer-ing from hair loss Wan-na knock your boss off Got a lit-tle
Pno.
G7
rub here for you Wan-na change e-mo-tion Try an an-cient po-tion Some e-xo-tic
Pno.

spoken
66
lo - tion All free for the tak - ing to you As long as you can af - for the price -
Pno.
Cmin
G7
70
DOB. & GREAT GAZ.
- - See 'The Great Ga - zoo - bees' And bet - ter your life Take a - way pain
Cmin
Cmin
G7
77
Take a - way strife See "The Great Ga - zoo - bees' And bet - ter your life
Cmin
Cmin
G7
83
He's the on - ly man to do it for you See 'The Great Ga - zoo - bees' And bet - ter your

C min
C min
life Take a - way pain Take a - way strife See 'The Great Ga - zoo - bees' And
Pno.
G 7
C min
THE GREAT GAZOOMBEES
bet - ter your life He's the on - ly man to do it for you Some - thing for the
Pno.
G 7
week - end Fol - low - ing the new trend Go on have a big spend Gua - ran - tedd to
Pno.
spoken
C min
DOB. & GREAT GAZ.
work with - in days by which time we - ll be gone See 'The Great Ga - zoo - bees' And
Pno.

G7
Cmin
Cmin
113
bet - ter your life Take a - way pain Take a - way strife See 'The Great Ga -
Pno.
G7
120
zoo - bees' And bet - ter your life He's the on - ly man to do He's the on - ly man to
Pno.
Cmin
126
do He's the on - ly man to do it for you
Pno.

Score

Malady

Song 3: (Act 1, Sc5)

Music and Lyrics by Jez Bond
Arrangement by Dimitri Scarlato

E♭maj7 F B♭ F E♭maj7 F B C♯
bo-dy can-not mend as the sea - son change she may ne-ver rise a-gain for her eyes are glazed and the
Vox. 2
Pno.
rit.
C♯min7 F♯13 G7 F♯7
fe-ver's in her brain She can ba-rely say her name...
Vox. 1
What, the fe-ver's in the brain But our
Vox. 2
Pno.
a tempo
C♯min7 F♯7 B C♯min7 F♯7 Badd9
Vox. 1
ba - by, our heir our one and on - ly To be born from out of all this strife Such a
Pno.

23
G♯7 C♯min F♯7 C♯min F♯
Though her
Vox. 1
dark dark day should be filled with so much joy not the ques - tions of death o - ver life
Pno.
27
B F♯ Emaj7 F♯ B F♯ Emaj7 F♯
heart is strong there is no-thing we can do though the day is long it is clear she'oo not pull through we will
Vox. 1
Pno.
31
C D Dmin7 G13 rit. A♭7 G7
loose her soon We will loose her and the chil Both the mo-ther and the child
Vox. 1
What, the mo-ther and the child? Both the mo-ther and the child
GREAT GAZOOMBEES & DOBSON
Vox. 2
Both the mo-ther and the child
Pno.

a tempo
C G Fmaj7 G
If I knew from whence all this ma - la - dy de - rived Then a
spoken
Vox. 1
Is there no cure, Doc-tor?
Vox. 2
Feel-ing joy - ous, feel - ing hap - py It seems my plan is work - ing
Pno.
C G Fmaj7 G Db Eb Ebmin7
cure might be with - in sight It de - fies all science, nei-ther fea - tures on my shelf I have
and soon the king-dom will be mine
rit.
Ab13 A7 Ab7 Db a tempo Ab
failed you my liege this night. Now her life does wane there is
spoken
GREAT GAZOOMBEES
DOBSON
GREAT GAZOOMBEES
You see Do - bo. What do con men do? Lie. Lie. ah

46
Gbmaj7 Ab Db Ab Gbmaj7 Ab
no - thing more to say I shall ease her pain I shall help sir each day
Vox. 1
uh
Can you
Vox. 2
uh
46
Pno.
49
D E Emin7 A13
rit.
Bb7 A7
it could be a while I shall take my leave.
D E
Vox. 1
say how long I sim - ply can - not say
Vox. 2
49
Pno

Score

Partners

Song 4: (Act1, Sc6)

Music and Lyrics by Jez Bond

Arrangement by Dimitri Scarlato

Blues ♩ = c. 142

E7
li - ving as two
I miss you when you're gone
Pno.
F♯
Be hard a - chiev - ing all the things that we do
If we were on - ly one
Pno.
E7 B♮7 E7
Part - ners, what it's all a - bout
Part - ners, what a team
Pno.
B♮7 E7 D♯7 D7 D♯7 E7 C♯min7 F♯7
Part - ners we're the per - fect pair
A part - ner - ship - ping dream
Pno.

B♮7
E7
I put the 'i' in-to a ma-gi-cal touch You put the 'u' in fraud
Pno.
F♯
Being a-lone I did-n't like much With you I'm ne-ver bored
Pno.
B♮7
E7
What is a ca-pa-wa with on-ly tow cars It's like a flight-less bird
Pno.
F♯
What is a deck chair but with-out a-ny decks It's to-tal-ly ab-surd
Pno.

E7
B♭7
Part - ners, what it's all a - bout
Pno.
E7
B♭7
E7
D♯7
D7
D♯7
E7
Part-ners, wha a team
Part-ners we're the per - fect team A
Pno.
C♯min7
F♯7
Swing - half tempo!
E7
B♭7
part - ner - ship - ping dream
Part - ners, what it's all a - bout
Pno.
E7
B♭7
E7
D♯7
D7
D♯7
E7
Part-ners, what a team
Part-ners we're the per - fect pair A
Pno.

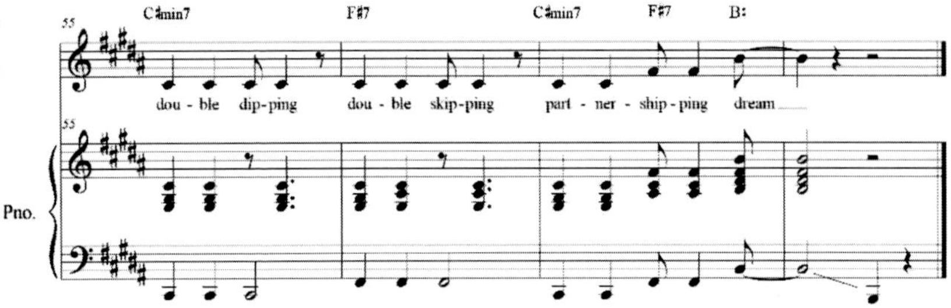
55
C♯min7
F♯7
C♯min7
F♯7
B:
dou - ble dip-ping dou - ble skip-ping part - ner - ship - ping dream
55
Pno.

We Were Meant to Be

Song 5: (Act 1, Sc9)

Music and Lyrics by Jez Bond
Arrangement by Dimitri Scarlato

13
F
B♭maj7
Csus
This per - fect part of me This part of me has gone
Pno.
17
Fadd9
Dmin7
B♭add9
Yes we were meant to be to - ge - ther
Pno.
21
Csus
Fadd9
Dmin7
B♭add9
All through the days and night for - e - ver
Pno.
25
Csus
Dmin
Dmin/C
B♭min
Then some day you'll find me Then some day you'll hold me
Pno.

29
C
Fadd9
Cmin7
F
Play - ing in tree - tops You'll sing and
Pno.
33
A♭maj7
F
B♭maj7
Csus
run But who'll be there for you When the day is
Pno.
37
Fadd9
Cmin7
F
done? Skat - ing with mum - my As the snow
Pno.
41
A♭maj7
F
B♭maj7
Csus
falls Will be with some - one else Some - one who's not
Pno.

Fadd9 Dmin7
yours Yes we were meant to be to -
Pno.
B♭add9 Csus Fadd9
ge - ther All through the days and night
Pno.
Dmin7 B♭add9 Csus Dmin
for - e - ver Then some day you'll find me
Pno.
Dmin/C B♭min C Fadd9
Then some day you'll hold me Though we are meant to be to -
KING GERARD
She'll have her mo - ther's heart
Pno.

61
B♭add9
C sus
ge-ther All through the days and night for - e - ver Though we are
Her strength and grace Her wit and charm Her no-ble face She'll have her
Pno.
67
Fadd9
B♭add9
meant to be to - ge-ther All through the days and night for-
mo - ther's eyes That look so rare Her warmth and grace
Pno.
73
Dmin
Dmin/C
e - ver Then some day you'll find me Then some day you'll
Some flow - ing hair some day I will find you
Pno.

B♭min
Fadd9
Cmin7
F
hold me
Be good to o - thers
As you ex -
some day I will hold you
Pno.
A♭maj7
F
B♭maj7
Csus
spoken
pect them to be
But if you call my name
Oh, Ge - rard.
Pno.

Score

Rapunzel - Park Theatre 2015

How Can I Be Yours

Song 6: (Act 2, Sc1)

Music and Lyrics by Jez Bond

Arrangement by Dimitri Scarlato

13
A D F♯min E Dmaj7
scared for you I don't know the jour - ney that you're go - ing on
Pno.
16
E Amaj7 D
May - be I'll be yours
Pno.
19
A E/B A/C♯ A E D E
We could be to - ge - ther May - be you'll be fright ned and a -
Pno.
22
A A/G♯ F♯min E D E
larmed Then you'll re - co gnise me there stand - ing o - pern armed Yes I
Pno.

A D F#min E A D
see you there Close e - nough to hold me And I need you here
Pno.
F# E A D F#min E
Wrap me in your arms But I'm scared for you I don't know the jour - ney that you're
Pno
Dmaj7 E C#7
go - ing on I be - lieve your heart is
Pno.
F#min F#7 Bmin
pure But I'm scared it's been frac - ture and torn a - part like a
Pno

37
E7 Amaj7 D
bro - ken heart May - be you're not there
Pno.
40
A E/B A/C♯ A E D E
May - be it's de - lu - sion
Just a stub - born man who'd ne - ver
Pno.
43
A A/G♯ F♯min E D E
stop
Just a fool - ish fa - ther who could not face gi ving up
Is it
Pno.
46
A D F♯min E A D
o - ver now? Pe - raphs I feel you've fad - ed
for the years have passed with-
Pno.

49
F♯
E
A
D
F♯min
E
no - thing e - ver changed I must take my plans Fare-well to this on - ly on - ly
Pno.
52
Dmaj7
E
Fmaj7
Gadd9
Aadd9
child of mine Fare - well to the child tha ne - ver was
Pno.

Score

Getting to know you

Song 7: (Act2, Sc2)

Music and Lyrics by Jez Bond
Arrangement by Dimitri Scarlato

G C F G C7
mine so then I'd hard - ly e - ven care Get-ting to know you, you and I to - ge - ther We'll be
Pno.
Bbmaj7 C13 F Bb F Dmin/G G
brav - ing a - ny wea - ther come what may Get-ting to know you, hold - ing hands and walk - ing We'll be
Pno.
C G C F G C7
talk - ing and I'll love the things you say Get-ting to know you sail - ing on for - e - ver There will
Pno.
Bbmaj7 C13 F Bb A Bb G7#5 C
ne - ver be an - oth - er lone - ly day For get-ting to know you means my life will be a dream and that you'll
Pno.
G7 C F
ne - ver e - ver go a - way. There's so much to tell I hard - ly know yout hi - sto-ry I
Pno.

B♭ F C A Dmin
listen as you tell me of you youth Then I tell you all of mine but really everything is fine because to-
Pno.
G C F
gether's always better yes forwife We'll grow old and walk with sticks and fall asleep more On that
Pno.
B♭ F C A
blanket where we snuggled underneath Then you'll turn and call me Geoff and then re-
Pno.
Dmin G C F G
peat it cause I'm deaf before you hand me that big jar with my false teeth Getting to know you,
Pno.
C7 B♭maj7 C13 F B♭ F
you and I together We'll be braving any weather come what may Getting to know you,
Pno.

Dmin/G G C G C F G
holding hands and walking we'll be talking and I'll love the things you say Getting to know you
Pno.
C7 B♭maj7 C13 F B♭ A B♭ G7♯5
sailing on for-e-ver There will ne-ver be an-oth-er lone-ly day For get-ting to know you means my
Pno.
C G7 C
life will be a dream and that you'll ne-ver e-ver go a-way. Yes get-ting to
Pno.
B♭ A B♭ G7♯5 C G7 C
know you means my life will be a dream and that you'll ne-ver e-ver go a-way.
Pno.

Score

Set Me Free

Song 8: (Act 2, Sc3)

Music and Lyrics by Jez Bond,
Awsa Bergstrom and Ian Dench
Arrangement by Dimitri Scarlato

37 Fmin Eb Db Eb
There's more that I wan-na know Set me Free Let me Go
41 Fmin Eb Db Db
Ex - plore the world down be - low Let me go
45 Ab Fmin Eb Db
oh oh oh oh oh oh oh oh oh oh oh oh oh oh
49 Bbmin Db Db
Mt dad - dy keeps me here in - side But
53 Ab Eb
what if all he told me is a lie
57 Bbmin Db Ab Eb
Is the world so ve - ry cruel Or
61 Bbmin Db Ab Eb
am I just his one and on - ly prize
65 Db Abmaj7/C Bbmin7 Bbmin7
If I had a hun - dred tons of steel and a wel - ding torch I could build
69 Abadd9 Abadd9 Ebsus Eb
a bridge from here to the world out - side Set me Free
73 Ab Fmin Eb Db
Let me Go There's more that I wan-na know Set me Free

77
Eb Fmin Eb Db
Let me Go Ex - plore the world down be - low
81
Db Ab Fmin Eb
Let me go oh oh oh oh oh oh oh oh oh oh oh oh
85
Db Fmin Db
oh oh Go! Feel the roar of thun - der Go! Can't stay one
89
Bbmin Eb
day lon - ger Go! I can make it on my own,
93
E A
here's a stone Set me Free Let me Go
97
F#min E D E
There's more that I wan-na know Set me Free Let me Go
101
F#min E D D
Ex - plore the world down be - low Let me go
105
A F#min E D
oh oh oh oh oh oh oh oh oh oh oh oh oh oh Let me go
109
A F#min E D
oh oh oh oh oh oh oh oh oh oh oh oh oh oh Let me go

113
A
F♯min
E
D
oh oh oh__ oh oh oh oh__ oh oh oh oh__ oh oh oh Let me go
117
A
F♯min
E
D
Fmin
oh oh oh__ oh oh oh oh__ oh oh oh oh__ oh oh oh Let me go

Score

Rapunzel - Park Theatre 2015

Ligthning Storm

Song 9: (Act 2, Sc6)

Music and Lyrics by Jez Bond
Arrangement by Dimitri Scarlato

C♯min C♯min/B A G♯7 C♯min C♯min/B F♯7/A♯ F♯7
heart's con-trol May-ve I can be your thun-der-bolt
Pno.
Amaj7 E E/G♯ A B
Light-ing ne-ver strikes the same place Grab this chance to start the race to - ge-ther
See-ing you is thril-ling Hold-ing you so chil-ling
Pno.
C♯min C♯min/B Amaj7 B E E/G♯ A B
Feel-ing you with-in me like a whirl-wind Think-ing words then talk-ing Step-ping out and walk-ing
Pno.

25
C♯min C♯min/B Amaj7 B E Emaj7 E
A lightn-ing storm Stron-ger than you'll
E-very stage I trem-ble like the leaves be-neath the wind A lightn-ing storm Stron-ger than you'll
ALL
Vox.
A lightn-ing storm Stron-ger than you'll
25
Pno.

29
D♯min7 G♯7 C♯min C♯min/B A G♯7
e - ver know Takes a-way your heart's con-trol May-ve I can be your thun-der-bolt
e - ver know Takes a-way your heart's con-trol May-ve I can be your thun-der-bolt
Vox.
e - ver know Takes a-way your heart's con-trol May-ve I can be your thun-der-bolt
29
Pno.

33
C♯min C♯min/B F♯7/A♯ F♯7 Amaj7
Light-ing ne-ver strikes the same place Grab this chance to start the race..... to-
Light-ing ne-ver strikes the same place Grab this chance to start the race.....
Vox.
Light-ing ne-ver strikes the same place Grab this chance to start the race.....
33
Pno.
37
E E/G♯ A B C♯min C♯min/B A B
ge-ther Nib-ble on your Nob-son Like a fedge with-in a crall
Dib-ble on your Dob-son Gib-ble on my mam-pass
37
Pno.
41
E E/G♯ A B C♯min C♯min/B A B
I feel it in my De-be And I'll place them in my podge A
She's giv-ing me a Se-be Touch my hang-ing Jack-son A
41
Pno.

E Emaj7 E D♯min7 G♯7
lightn-ing storm Stron-ger than you'll e - ver know Takes a-way your
lightn-ing storm Stron-ger than you'll e - ver know Takes a-way your
Vox.
lightn-ing storm Stron-ger than you'll e-ver know
Pno.

C♯min C♯min/B A G♯7 C♯min C♯min/B F♯7/A♯ F♯7
heart's con-trol May-ve I can be your thun-der-bolt
heart's con-trol May-ve I can be your thun-der-bolt
Vox.
Takes a-way your heart's con - trol
Pno.

53
Amaj7
E Emaj7 Amaj7
Light-ing ne-ver strikes the same place Grab this chance to start the race to - ge-ther You and me to-
Light-ing ne-ver strikes the same place Grab this chance to start the race to - ge-ther You and me to-
Vox.
Light - - - Grab to - ge-ther
Pno.

57
E Emaj7
E/B B E
ge - ther we'll be a light - a light - ing storm
ge - ther we'll be a light - a light - ing storm
Vox.
we'll be a light - ing storm
Pno.